Transcriptions • Lessons • Tips • Photos

25 GREAT BASS LINES

Featuring Pop, Rock, Funk, and R&B Bass Guitar Legends, Including James Jamerson, Paul McCartney, Bootsy Collins, Jack Bruce, Flea, Donald "Duck" Dunn, John Entwistle, George Porter, Jr., Roger Waters, and Many More

by Glenn Letsch

ALSO AVAILABLE:

| Stuff! Good Bass Players Should Know HL00696014 | Hal Leonard R&B Bass Method HL00695823 | Bass for Beginners HL00695099 | James Brown Bass Signature Licks HL00696022 |

Paul McCartney and Bootsy Collins cover photos © Photofest.

Jack Bruce, George Porter, Jr. and Roger Waters cover photos © Retna Ltd.

Flea cover photo by Marty Temme.

PLAYBACK+
Speed • Pitch • Balance • Loop

To access audio visit:
www.halleonard.com/mylibrary

"Enter Code"
7792-6293-4606-8115

ISBN 978-1-4234-6056-5

T0057706

Visit Hal Leonard Online at
www.halleonard.com

Contact us:
Hal Leonard
7777 West Bluemound Road
Milwaukee, WI 53213
Email: info@halleonard.com

In Europe, contact:
Hal Leonard Europe Limited
42 Wigmore Street
Marylebone, London, W1U 2RN
Email: info@halleonardeurope.com

In Australia, contact:
Hal Leonard Australia Pty. Ltd.
4 Lentara Court
Cheltenham, Victoria, 3192 Australia
Email: info@halleonard.com.au

Preface

25 Great Bass Lines consists of some of the greatest bass lines ever recorded in popular music history. A wide variety of bassists, bands, and styles have been included, but the one common thread that connects them all is that each great bass line anchors a great song. Beginning with the British Invasion of the early 1960s with the Beatles' "All My Loving" and the Zombies' "She's Not There," then moving to American R&B with Junior Walker's "(I'm a) Road Runner" and the Capitols' "Cool Jerk," the '60s are heavily represented. The music of this era is, after all, musical bedrock for electric bass players.

The 1970s are also dominant, when bass playing became more sophisticated as songwriting evolved. "Get Up (I Feel Like Being a) Sex Machine" by James Brown can challenge the best of us and Marvin Gaye's "What's Going On" is an absolute musical masterpiece by the great James Jamerson. The Who's "Won't Get Fooled Again" and "Free Ride" by the Edgar Winter Group will challenge any bassist to learn how to drive a song without getting in the way. Great bass playing is like a high wire act: there is a fine line between the aerialist dancing on the wire (and bassist dancing through a song) and the aerialist losing his balance (and the bassist overplaying and destroying the song).

The '80s and '90s are touched on as well with contributions from Queen's "Another One Bites the Dust," the B-52's "Love Shack," and the Red Hot Chili Peppers' "Aeroplane."

All these songs groove hard, so if you learn them all, your groove will be closer to mastery. So, without further delay, let's get started.

Acknowledgments

Thank you to my wife Anne and daughter Alysia for their support and guidance.

Thank you to David Hood, Andy Fraser, Chris White, Colin Blunstone, Bootsy Collins, Bob Babbitt, George Porter, Jr., Pete Thompson, Brian Brinkerhoff, and Masaki Liu.

About the Audio

The accompanying audio with this book includes all 25 bass lines performed note for note with a full band. With PLAYBACK+ software, you can adjust the recording to any tempo without changing pitch!

Glenn Letsch: bass, guitar, percussion
Jason White: drums, percussion
John Mader: drums, percussion
Justin Garns: guitars
Jeff Tamelier: guitars
Thomas Suczek: keyboards
Rock Hendrix: saxophones

Contents

Paul McCartney

© Photofest

"All My Loving" is the very first song I ever heard by the Beatles. Already a smash in England and Europe, they were a brand new attraction to America in early 1964. We were still reeling from the assassination of JFK in November of 1963 and didn't take notice of the Beatles until after Christmas. Ed Sullivan was aware of them though, and he brought them to America the first chance he got. On the February 9, 1964, the Beatles appeared on *The Ed Sullivan Show* at 8:00 Sunday night. The whole country watched; the teenage girls fainted. When they appeared on the TV screen and Paul began singing, "Close your eyes," it was all over for me. I decided half way through "All My Loving" that I was going to take up guitar and bass and start a rock band. Looking back 40 plus years, it was truly a life changing moment.

The Beatles are the biggest band of all time. Formed in England in 1960, there's probably not a single adult in America today that cannot name the Fab Four's members. Considering this, I won't list their innumerous accomplishments, except the fact that they have sold over a billion records. Sir James Paul McCartney was born on June 18, 1942. He is the most successful songwriter in music history, winning too many awards and selling too many records to count. His influential bass playing is sometimes overshadowed by his greater musicality in general. With that said, he is also one of the finest bass players ever. His sense of rhythm, melody, harmony, and counterpoint puts him in a class by himself.

"All My Loving" is an excellent example of a McCartney bass masterpiece (and there are many, many more). Apparently conceived as a poem for his girlfriend, Jane Asher, while he was shaving, it was the first of only a few occasions where McCartney wrote the lyrics before the music. Interestingly, Paul originally envisioned it as a country tune. The Beatles recorded the song on July 30, 1963 in eleven takes with three overdubs; remixing took place a few weeks later. Upon release at the end of 1962, it promptly drew critical acclaim and received heavy radio rotation.

McCartney sang lead and double-tracked his vocal to bring it out in the mix. George Harrison's countrified solo, heavily influenced by his idol Chet Atkins, became a favorite among guitar fans, and John Lennon's triplet-based chordal strumming

This Beatles classic was never released as a single, but it was the first song the group played on their first Ed Sullivan Show appearance: February 9, 1964. It was a historic telecast, as over 73 million people tuned in.

propels the song nicely. The bass playing, though, is the musical centerpiece. Paul plays a wonderful descending walking bass line through the ii–V–I (F#m–B–E) chord progression. It creates symmetry and balance, as he sings an ascending melody in contrast. The fact that he sang the lead vocal *while* playing the bass line is remarkable.

McCartney is not only a singing bass player; he's in tune with the entire range of the song. He has clear and concise ideas about guitar parts (and often plays them), keyboard parts (and often plays them!), and drum parts (and often plays those too!). He's a complete musician and has earned the respect of his peers in many more ways than one. What he accomplished with "All My Loving" was only the beginning, but what an amazing beginning it was. It was like hitting a grand slam homerun your first time at bat in Major League Baseball. The thing is, he seemed to do that nearly every time he sang and played bass for the Beatles.

How to Play It

Much of the bass line to this song makes use of the E major scale in open position. Keep your fretting hand in first position (first finger at fret 1, second finger at fret 2, etc.). There are four sharps in the key of E major: F#, C#, G#, D#. Ascend starting from the low open E to F# and G# on string 4. Now play A, B, and C# on string 3. Finally, play D# and E on string 2. Now descend the same way you ascended.

Once you've learned that fingering, try descending the E major scale starting at F# on string 2, which is two frets above E. So you'll be descending F#, E, D#, C#, B, A, G#, F#, and the open E. Do this several times until it becomes instinctive.

Next, play the first four notes of what you just played: F#, E, D#, and C#. You've just played the four-note routine to accompany the first chord of the song: F# minor, the ii chord. Continue on with the next four notes of the scale: B, A, G#, and F#. That's the four-note pattern for the second chord of the song: B, the V chord. You have just played a classic *walking bass* line.

Walking Bass 101

There are many ways to walk a bass line. This is the most foolproof way, and it makes you sound as if you know what you're doing. When you have one chord per measure (in 4/4 time), start on the root and ascend or descend the key's scale for the first three notes. For example, in the key of E major, over an F#m chord, you could play F#–E–D# (descending) or F#–G#–A (ascending). The fourth note is the most important note. You need to play a chord tone (F#m is spelled F#–A–C#), and make sure that chord tone is either a half step (one fret) or a whole step (two frets) above or below the root of the following chord—in this case, B. You have two choices: C#, which is a whole step above the root (B) of B7, or A, which is a whole step below it.

There are other ways to walk on the bass, but this method works every time. You should become thoroughly proficient with this method before you move on to other walking methods. Lucky for you, "All My Loving" is an excellent song on which to practice. It follows Walking Bass 101 to the letter (or note). It also tastefully injects a few other musical ideas to keep things fresh and interesting. Walking up and down the scale tones can get pretty monotonous.

In measure 3, Paul stops walking the scale and plays an E major arpeggio (E–G#–B–E). In measure 4, he scales this routine

down to just the root (C#) and 5th (G#) of C# minor. He repeats this procedure (arpeggio for one measure and root/5th for the next) for the A and F#m chords in measures 5 and 6, respectively. Finally, he concludes his phrase with roots only for the D and B7 chords. Measures 9–16 are almost identical, but the progression changes to A–B–E–E for the final four measures. He treats the A chord as he previously did and resumes walking on the B, playing the same exact line as he did in measure 2. McCartney wraps things up in measure 15 with a descending E6 arpeggio (E–C#–B–G#), where E is the root, C# is the major 6th, B is the perfect 5th, and G# is the major 3rd.

McCartney had the most amazing knack for playing exactly what the song called for. It's just about impossible to improve upon his choice of bass line. If you don't believe me, go ahead and try!

Vital Stats

Bassist: Paul McCartney

Song: "All My Loving"

Album: *Meet the Beatles –* The Beatles, 1963

Age at time of recording: 21

Bass: Hofner violin bass

Amp: Miked Tannoy Dual-Concentric (15" speaker and cabinet) driven by a Leak Point One preamp and Leak TL-12 Plus amplifier

Track 1

Verse
Moderately fast ♩ = 157

Chris White

"Apart from being a brilliant songwriter and bass player, Chris was a great character on stage and also had great stage presence."
—The Zombies lead vocalist, Colin Blunstone

© Getty

The Zombies were an English rock band formed in 1959 in St. Albans. Their hits in the USA during the mid and late sixties were "She's Not There," "Tell Her No," and "Time of the Season." Their 1968 album *Odessey and Oracle*, written by the group's principal songwriters, Rod Argent and Chris White, is ranked #80 on *Rolling Stone* magazine's list of the 500 Greatest Albums of All Time.

After winning a competition sponsored by the London Evening News, the Zombies signed a record contract with Decca Records. Their first and greatest hit, "She's Not There," was keyboardist Rod Argent's second song ever and was written specifically for this recording session.

Released in 1964, it peaked at #12 in the UK, where it was their only Top 40 hit. Stan Z. Burns first aired the song in the USA a few months later during his daily noontime "Hot Spot" with the New York City rock station WINS. The tune began to catch on in early fall and eventually climbed to #2.

The main instrument of "She's Not There" is a Hohner Pianet, which had a very haunting tonal quality that was unusual for the time. The tune is a minor key, jazzy number, distinguished by Argent's Pianet, Colin Blunstone's breathy vocal,

close harmony backing vocals, and Chris White's moody but powerful bass. The song was unlike anything heard in British rock music at the time. By the time they hit #3 in the USA with "Time of the Season," the band had already broken up, and Argent had started his own group.

Bassist Chris White recalls how the song came together: "When we were rehearsing 'She's Not There' in my bedroom at home, Rod played the song through, and he had this great left hand part which was in the chords already. I copied the part because it sounded great, and that was the start of the whole bass part. From there, I just tried different feels for the other two sections of the song. The combination of bass and left-hand Pianet became a feature of our sound after that."

I remember the year 1964 vividly. When "She's Not There" came on the radio for the first time in August, it knocked me out. After the first chorus, the bass takes a one-measure solo. Once I heard that, I *had* to figure out that bass line. I was just a beginner and asked for help from a guitar player friend. He got close, but he ended up showing me a part that moved with the chords on the Hohner Pianet. He missed the whole point of why the bass line grabs you and pulls you into the song: the bass does *not* change with the chords. By not moving with the changes, the bass creates *tension*. This very tension elevates the bass line from musical competence to artistic brilliance. Even to this day, young, aspiring bassists come to me asking how to play "She's Not There." I never get tired of listening to this song, and I become inspired to teach it whenever asked to do so.

"She's Not There" was the Zombies' first single. They also recorded Gershwin's "Summertime," which was supposed to be the band's first single, but "She's Not There" got the nod.

How to Play It

If you think of these bass phrases in the main verse as chord arpeggios, you'll learn to play this part quickly and understand it more thoroughly as well. Refer to the notation and tablature. When you *arpeggiate* a chord, you play the notes one at a time. This is a popular bass technique, because if you strum full chords on the bass, the notes become undistinguishable. Try to avoid any single note accidentally sustaining into the next. This too will make your bass part muddy. With such a great line, each note deserves to be heard clearly and cleanly.

Let's start with the A and E in the first half of the first measure. Think of this as an Am chord; you're playing the octave (pickup note), the root, and the perfect 5th of the chord. This is followed with D and F♯, which should be thought of as the root (D) and the major 3rd (F♯) of a D chord. This is followed by an E, which acts as the 5th of the Am chord as the pattern repeats. A similar pattern is played for the verse, but note that the F♯ is lowered to F♮ to coincide with the F major chord in measures 7 and 11.

Next comes the pre-chorus section beginning in measure 13. The bass plays single notes against each chord in the first measure: F♯ is the major 3rd of the D chord, and F♮ is the minor 3rd of the Dm chord. Chris outlines the Am chord in measure 14, follows with a root/5th routine on the Em chord, and arpeggiates the Am again afterwards. He sticks to the root for the C chord in measure 18 and anticipates the E7 chord by a half step

before pounding out solid eighth note E notes in anticipation of the chorus.

The chorus section is next. The bass clearly follows the roots of the chords, with the exception of the D, where Chris also includes the major 3rd (F♯). The big payoff occurs at the end of the section, which could be called a bass "solo." As the band stops, the bass plows ahead with a line based off the A minor pentatonic scale: A–C–D–E–G (though the G note is not included). After all these years, it still sounds so brilliant.

Vital Stats

Bassist: Chris White

Song: "She's Not There"

Album: *The Zombies –* The Zombies, 1964

Age at time of recording: 21

Bass: John Bacon hand made bass, Harpenden, UK

Amp: Miked homemade bass amp combined with direct into the mixing console

She's Not There

Intro
Moderately ♩ = 130

Verse

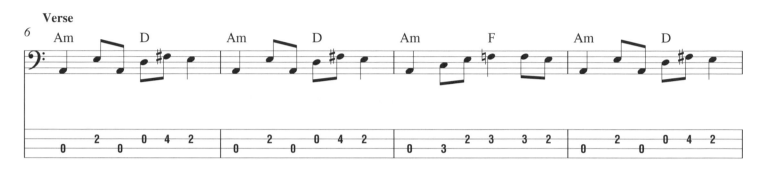

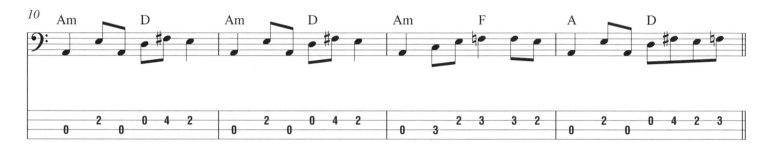

Pre-Chorus

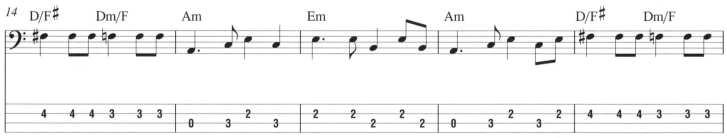

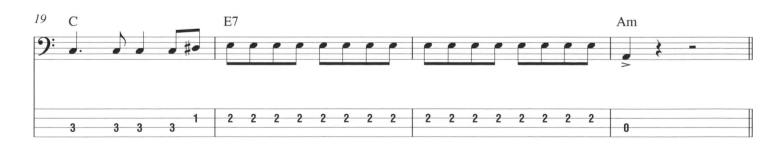

Words and Music by Rod Argent

James Jamerson

"I picked up things from listening to people speak— the intonation of their voices; I could capture a line. I look at people walking and get a beat from their movement."

—James Jamerson

© Getty

"(I'm a) Road Runner" was recorded by Junior Walker & the All-Stars in 1965 and was originally released on their debut album, *Shotgun*. It was so successful a tune that they released it again on their follow-up album, *Roadrunner*, in 1966. Although "How Sweet It Is (To Be Loved by You)" surpassed it in two out of three charts, "(I'm a) Road Runner" is no less a fan favorite from Junior Walker & the All-Stars. The song made it to #20 on the pop singles charts, but it's had serious staying power, as it still appears in radio rotation. The song has been covered by Peter Frampton and Fleetwood Mac, among others.

Junior Walker was born Autry DeWalt Mixon in 1931. With Walker's saxophone as the signature of their sound, he and the All-Stars were signed to Motown Records in the early sixties and became one of their marquee bands. The other members of the group were James Graves on drums, Willie Woods on guitar, and Vic Thomas on keys.

Their first hit, "Shotgun," is considered their signature song and went to #4 on the Hot 100 chart. Their other big hit was "Shake and Fingerpop." Most of their songs were vehicles to let Junior Walker rip on his tenor sax, with the exception of "What Does It Take (To Win Your Love)" in 1969, which made it to the top 5 on the singles chart and featured more singing than sax.

In 1981, Junior was asked to play on Foreigner's hit single "Urgent." His brilliant work on the song was actually comped from a series of takes at the recording session. Mutt Lange produced the session in collaboration with the band's leader, Mick Jones. For something cobbled together, the track sounds incredibly natural.

Junior Walker passed away in 1995 at the age of 64 in Battle Creek, Michigan from cancer. He was posthumously inducted into the Rhythm and Blues Foundation later that year. Drummer James Graves died tragically in 1967 in a car accident, and guitarist Willie Woods died in 1997 at age 60. Junior Walker & the All-Stars' biggest hit, "Shotgun," was inducted into the Grammy Hall of Fame in 2002.

Since there was no official bassist in the band, James Jamerson was frequently asked to play on their recordings for Motown. In addition to "Shotgun," which is much less predictable than it appears, "Home Cookin'" is another tune on which James tears it up. "(I'm a) Road Runner" actually opens with a bass intro. How cool is that? James immediately grabs your ear right out of the gate. (See also "Bernadette," "For Once in My Life," and "What's Going On" for more James Jamerson background information.)

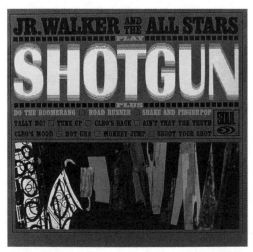

Junior Walker, whose real name was Autry DeWalt, was a saxophone player who made his vocal debut on "Shotgun." He recorded the vocals because the singer didn't show up, and the rest is history.

How to Play It

The song is in F, which puts us in first position on the bass. Place your first finger on the first fret. Most of the notes fall within the first three frets, but you'll occasionally need to accommodate a four-fret stretch. This particular bass routine has a strong incessant drive and never lets up. The notes need to sound the same in order to maintain this drive. Therefore, it's recommended you try plucking the whole song with the same finger. I prefer to use my second finger, as it's stronger, but use what's comfortable for you. In any event, feel free to try alternating fingers so you can discover for yourself what really sounds best. You will likely come to the same conclusion and opt for a single finger (or thumb) to play the whole song. It might be a bit more work at first, but it will open your ears to a deeper listen.

You'll discover that each song requires its own special technique to make it sound the way it needs to. To get that special sound or feel, you might need to pluck with one finger, use your thumb, or use a pick. You may even want to stuff some foam rubber under your strings near the bridge to cut down on sustain. It is important that your considerations be made on a song-by-song basis, as each song has its own unique personality.

The intro to "Road Runner" can almost be considered a bass solo; it's front and center. Refer to the notation and, more importantly, pay close attention to the tablature for accurate note location on the fingerboard. The notes Jamerson uses here come from the altered major blues scale. The use of open strings allows you to be economical with your hand movements. Stay off your fingertips and lean more towards your finger pads (where your fingerprints are). Keep your fingers close to the fretboard so they rest and mute the unused strings. If you play this part accurately, your fretting hand will barely appear to move, but the bass line will dance!

This tune can be deceptive. It appears simple, but the arrangement is surely not. Notice that each verse is comprised of several phrases that are all similar but slightly different. Each begins with F, but they diverge afterward. There are subtle shifts in the bass line during each pass through the verse. Jamerson never quite played the same phrase the same way twice. This makes the bass line breathe and keeps things interesting no matter how simple the line might appear.

Vital Stats

Bassist: James Jamerson

Song: "(I'm a) Road Runner"

Album: *Shotgun* – Junior Walker & the All Stars, 1965

Age at time of recording: 29

Bass: 1962 Sunburst, 1965 Fender Precision Bass ("The Funk Machine")

Amp: Recorded direct into the mixing console

Track 3

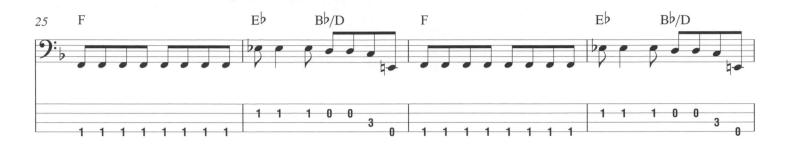

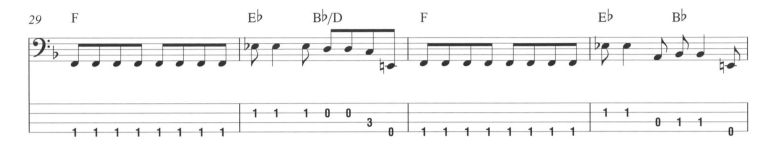

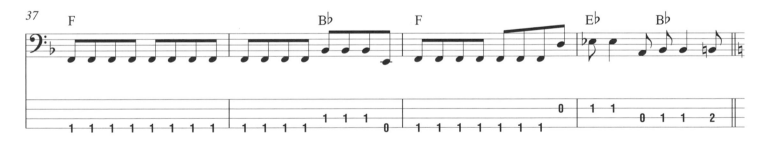

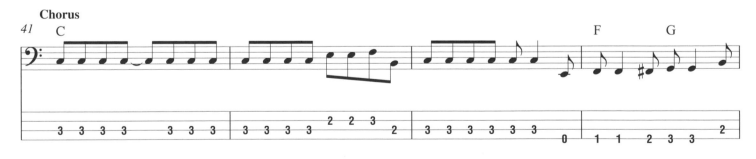

Chorus

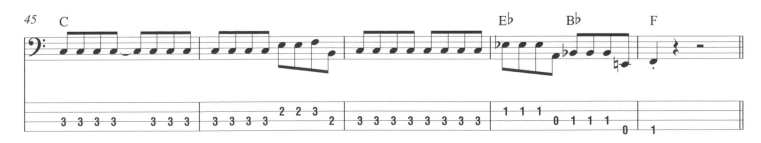

Tommy Cogbill

Of the numerous renditions, Wilson Pickett's version of "Mustang Sally" has become the standard to which all others are compared. Written by Mack Rice, this R&B blues song was first recorded by Mack in 1965. It gained its greatest popularity though when Wilson covered it in 1966. The song started as a joke when Della Reese's bandleader wanted a new Ford Mustang. Rice first called the song "Mustang Mama," but changed the title when Aretha Franklin came up with "Mustang Sally."

Pickett's version climbed to #6 R&B and #23 Pop in 1966. *Rolling Stone* ranked the song #434 on a list of the 500 Greatest Songs of All Time. To quote the magazine, "'Mustang Sally' nearly ended up on the studio floor—literally. After Pickett finished his final take at Fame Studios in Muscle Shoals, Alabama, the tape suddenly flew off the reel and broke into pieces. But the session engineer, the legendary Tom Dowd, calmly cleared the

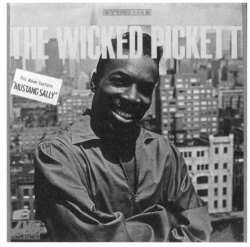

Writer Sir Mack Rice states that this song was originally titled "Mustang Mama," but was changed to "Mustang Sally" at the behest of Aretha Franklin.

Wilson Pickett

"Tommy Cogbill was a soft-spoken, laid-back guy, but with a bass in his hands, he had the intuitive ability to create forward motion through a song that enabled everyone else to surf in the wake."

—Nashville bassist Michael Rhodes

room and told everyone to come back in half an hour. Dowd pieced the tape back together and saved what became one of the funkiest soul anthems of the sixties. The staple of wedding and bar band set lists worldwide, it's as infectious today as it was in 1966.

The great Tommy Cogbill performs the bass line. An accomplished bebop guitar player long before becoming a renowned session bassist, Tommy was born in 1932 in Johnson Grove, Tennessee. He was a first call session musician for artists working in Nashville and Muscle Shoals, with a list of accomplishments that's envied by the best in the business. He played on "Funky Broadway," "Son of a Preacher Man," and many others. He recorded with Elvis Presley, Kris Kristofferson, J.J. Cale, Aretha Franklin, Chuck Berry, Bob Seger, and Neil Diamond, to name a few. He died too soon at age 50 in 1982 in Nashville, Tennessee.

How to Play It

The bass line, at a casual glance, appears to lie in a typical box pattern. By this I mean that the majority of the notes are played within an octave "box" (a three-fret stretch). Roots, 5ths, ♭7ths, octaves, and occasional perfect 4ths are weaved together in repeating patterns. Sometimes playing "in the box" results in a generic blues routine. This is hardly the case here.

The classic "Mustang Sally" bass line is one of the most misquoted bass lines in R&B history. I have never heard this bass part played correctly—either by a bar band or even on a newer recorded rendition. Most players who try to decipher the bass line do not hear the correct notes. Rather, they approach the song generically and try to process the bass line by employing a familiar pattern for their fretting hand (and their ear). This is a big mistake. They should be listening for what makes this song (and the bass line) special and unique. As a close listen will reveal, the notes in this song are not in all the familiar places.

Ear's the Story

A musician's first instrument should be his or her ear. The instrument he or she holds is their secondary instrument. If you accept this premise, you must train your ear before you can play your instrument effectively. We all need ear training to familiarize ourselves with the language of music.

For the sake of *feeling* this bass line, let's practice playing and *listening* to half-step intervals. First, alternate between C and B notes back and forth. Then, try *singing* the notes as you play them, George Benson-style. You don't have to *sound* like George, but be sure to hit the exact pitch so you can feel the note. Remember, this is for practice purposes only; it's not a concert performance. You need to intuitively feel how *different* these notes sound.

Next, alternate between C and B♭ the same way and sing those notes as well. Now, make a mental note of how different the C–B routine sounds from the C–B♭ routine. They aren't even close, are they? If you understand my point, then you're ready to tackle "Mustang Sally." It's time to bring the song to life. Rather than lower the bar to bar-band generic, let's raise it to studio-musician cool.

Keep in mind that these musicians were brought in to make hit songs because they were the best musicians around.

They were monster players with monster chops and diverse musical backgrounds. Producers called on them to make these tracks special because they could *deliver* on their instruments with unique creative energy while under the pressures of the recording studio. They avoided sounding generic like the plague.

This classic bass line starts with a simple, early country root–5th approach (C–G, C–G) but contains a few very hip twists. Chromatic approach tones are introduced (B–C and F♯–G) along with a syncopated upbeat feel. The A note is used as a connecting note after the F♯–G move to get back to the B note and begin the routine again. Low and behold, you have pure musical magic.

Factor in the rhythmic and harmonic counterpoint of the two guitar parts along with the drum pattern, and you have an undeniable musical hit that sounds as fresh as the day it came out nearly four decades ago. If you listen carefully, you'll notice the guitar using a half-step hammer-on approach as well. Maybe that was the catalyst for the bass player's line, or vice versa. What we do know is these cats had huge ears. They could *feel* what worked. Play this song with this heightened sense of musical awareness, and everyone in the joint will be jumpin'—guaranteed.

Vital Stats

Bassist: Tommy Cogbill

Song: "Mustang Sally"

Album: *The Wicked Pickett* – Wilson Pickett, 1966

Age at time of recording: 34

Bass: '60s Fender Precision Bass

Amp: 1960's piggyback Fender Bassman—no direct input used

Cool Jerk 1966

Bob Babbitt

"I played an early '60s Precision bass. I strung it with La Bella flatwounds and used a sponge to deaden the strings. When the strings got gunked up, I'd boil them in lemon water to bring them back to life."

—Bob Babbitt

© Marty Temme

Formed in 1962 and originally known as the Caps, the Capitols began as a trio on Motown Records. After signing with the Karen record label, the group went on to record and release their first single in 1963, "Dog and Cat" b/w "The Kick." After disappointing sales, the group dissolved.

The mid-1960s was a time of many dance crazes. One of the most popular was called "The Jerk," during which you held your arms out in different positions and made thrusting motions with your hips. A sexual version of the dance, called the "Pimp Jerk," soon became popular in Detroit. Don Storball and Julius Jones (both former Capitols)

seized the opportunity and wrote a song about the pimp jerk. They recorded at Golden World Studios in Detroit in March of 1966 with the legendary Motown house band, the Funk Brothers. Renamed "Cool Jerk" (so radio stations would not ban it), the song became a hit, reaching as high as #7 on the Hot 100 and #2 on the R&B charts, and the group re-formed.

Though the group had a short career, "Cool Jerk" has stood the test of time. It's been used in Cool Whip commercials and many movie soundtracks, including *More American Graffiti*, *Home Alone 2*, and *Calendar Girl*. The song has also made its share of "best of" lists, including 100 Greatest Rock Bass Performances (#70) and VH-1's 100 Greatest Dance Songs (#48). The song is still played in heavy rotation on radio stations across the world.

Bob Babbitt is a legendary bassist most famous for his work as a member of Motown's studio band, the Funk Brothers,

from 1966–1972. He traded off sessions with original Motown bassist, James Jamerson. Over the course of his career, Bob has played on over 200 hit songs, including "Signed, Sealed, Delivered," "War," "Tears of a Clown," "Mercy Mercy Me," "Ball of Confusion," "Midnight Train to Georgia," and many more. He also played on the Jimi Hendrix album, *Crash Landing*.

Bob comments about his early career: "I was a good sight-reader, but Golden World (where 'Cool Jerk' was recorded) was pretty loose. The guys at Motown had it a lot tougher, because it was more structured over there. I used to get accused of overplaying from time to time, but those problems faded as I matured. Listening to some of the great bassists who came into town to perform at the Minor Key (a jazz nightclub) helped me a lot. My influences at the time were Ray Brown, Charles Mingus, Paul Chambers, Monk Montgomery, and Jamerson. Ray Brown's *Bass Method* had a huge effect on me. Even though

I'm not really a jazz player, I picked up a lot of things from those guys. I once saw Mingus pop his G string on a gig, so I tried it on a Golden World session. The producer said, 'Don't ever do that again.' Of course, now everyone does it."

There was an interesting debate about who actually played bass on "Cool Jerk." Bob likes to tell the story of him and James Jamerson stopping for a drink after a long day in the recording studio. As they sat listening to the juke box ("Cool Jerk" was playing), James said to Bob, "Hear that?" Bob responded, "Yeah, I hear that, why?" Jamerson said, "Moi, me!" Bob retorted, "That's not you, that's me!" Apparently, Jamerson had played on an earlier version of the tune, but Bob was brought in to re-track the bass. It is more likely that the bass was re-cut for technical or arrangement purposes than any fault of Jamerson's. Things were moving fast and furious in those days at the Motown studios, and it was difficult indeed to keep up with who played on what song.

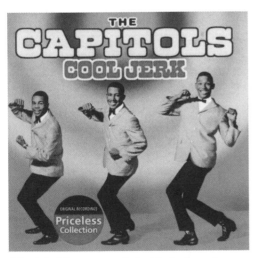

"Cool Jerk" was recorded with the legendary Motown house band the Funk Brothers. It was supposed to include a horn arrangement, but the contracted musicians failed to show up for the recording session and their parts were omitted from the track.

How to Play It

With a fierce backbeat fueling the groove, this song deserves utmost respect. Anyone who played *anything* on this track was at the top of their game, and every instrument contributed to the final, awesome product—tambourine, piano, drums, guitar, and the singers. This song must have given everyone chills listening back in the control room.

The tune is notated in "cut" time, which means we're counting 83 half notes per minute rather than 166 quarter notes per minute. This helps you avoid having to count at such a frantic pace. Tapping your foot at 166 beats per minute might not lend itself to a smooth groove.

"Cool Jerk" is in the key of E♭. One might expect this to be a hindrance for an electric bass, which is tuned to a low E. But the uniqueness of a high root (E♭) played against a piano, which is capable of a low E♭, actually widens the overall sonic feel. Plus, consider the sonic impact of the key of E♭ versus the key of E. It was no accident many of the great Motown tunes were recorded in flat keys.

The bass works off the dominant 7th chord to create a verse groove. The root (E♭) jumps down to the low major 3rd (G) and then climbs to the 5th (B♭) before finishing off with ♭7th (D♭) and the tonic (E♭). The scale in use here is the E♭ Mixolydian mode. Refer to the tablature for best fingering location. This same routine is transposed for the IV chord in measures 5–8.

The bridge moves to the iii (Gm) and vi (Cm) and brings things back around with the IV chord (A♭) and four measures on the V (B♭). The iii chord is decorated with a chromatic run, F–F♯–G, whereas the brief Cm chord is handled with two quarter-note jabs on the root. For the IV chord (A♭), the routine is similar to measures 5–8, but there's an additional chromatic note (D) placed before the E♭. For the V chord, the I-chord routine from the intro is transposed down a 4th. Notice, however, that Babbitt concludes this line with the low B♭, which has stronger impact and acts as an exclamation point tacked on to the end of the section.

The bass line grooves hard. As you play, try to feel the backbeat emphasized on the original recording by the snare drum, tambourine, handclaps, and guitar. Your part will really swing if you key off these instruments. Remember, your first instrument is your ear; that is what helps make you a more soulful musician. You must *listen* first, and then play.

Vital Stats

Bassist: Bob Babbitt

Song: "Cool Jerk"

Album: *Dance the Cool Jerk* – The Capitols, 1966

Age at time of recording: 24

Bass: Early '60s Cherry Red Fender Precision with a Jazz Bass neck

Amp: Recorded direct into the mixing console

Cool Jerk

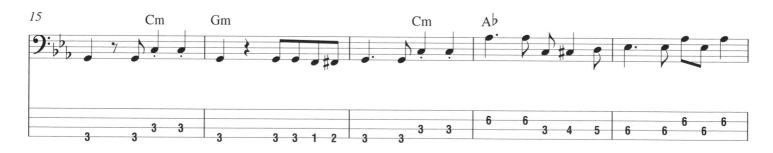

Words and Music by Donald Storball

James Jamerson

© Photofest

"He was the first melodic electric bass player— especially the Four Tops stuff. The bass on 'Bernadette' is serious. That is a hard bass line. There are still guys today who can't play that one. That gave me some trouble actually, because I used to play those parts on gigs."
—Stanley Clarke

"Bernadette" is a 1967 hit recorded by the Four Tops for the Motown label. Featured on the *Reach Out* album, it was written and produced by Motown's main production team of Holland-Dozier-Holland and is one of the most well-known Motown tunes of the sixties. It reached #4 on the Billboard Hot 100 and ended up being the band's final Top 10 hit of the decade.

The Four Tops' repertoire included jazz, soul, R&B, disco, doo-wop, adult contemporary, and even showtunes. Founding members Levi Stubbs, Duke Fakir, Obie Benson, and Lawrence Payton formed the group in Detroit during the early fifties. They remained together for over four decades, continuing without a single personnel change from 1953 until 1997. The band played a huge role in defining the Motown sound of the sixties. Part of their unique charm was the fact that lead singer Levi Stubbs was a baritone; groups of that era typically featured a tenor as the lead vocalist.

The Tops were the favorites of the legendary songwriting team Holland-Dozier-Holland, and they wrote a steady stream of hits for the group, including "I Can't Help Myself" and "Reach Out I'll Be There." The band continued together even after the Motown label left Detroit, signing with ABC Records, Casablanca, and Arista during their legendary run.

A change of lineup finally occurred when Lawrence Payton died in 1997. They continued as a three-piece known as the Tops, but added the fourth member when Theo Peoples of the Temptations joined. Levi Stubbs suffered a stroke in 2000, and Ronnie McNeir replaced him. In 2005, Benson passed away, and Payton's son, Roquel, replaced him. As of 2006, the Four Tops were still performing.

James Jamerson was born in 1936 and performed on the majority of the Four Tops recordings. This is largely unknown because he wasn't credited on the albums (as was the case with all the Motown session players until 1971). He is widely regarded as one of the most influential bassists in history and is known as the "Father of Modern Bass Guitar." James was inducted into the Rock and Roll Hall of Fame posthumously in 2000.

There are many great bass players today with chops beyond that of Jamerson's. But chops alone do not make you *musical*. You certainly do need technical mastery of your instrument, but you also need an intuitive sense of melody, counterpoint, harmony, and most importantly, a highly refined sense of rhythm (a natural feel for the funky groove). James could play around the melody and *never ever* get in the way of the song. His playing could be busy or laid back, but it *always* served the song. This is why James was *always* working during the Motown days. When he was unavailable, other bassists were hired to play like him. James Jamerson set the bar, and few could measure up.

I first heard "Bernadette" on an old-fashioned jukebox at a neighborhood pizza parlor as a senior in high school back in 1967. Those old boxes had tons of bass because there were two 15"

The Four Tops went 41 years without any member changes (1956–1997). Levi Stubbs was their lead vocalist. He was a baritone, which was rare, as the lead was usually a tenor.

speakers inside the compartment below the record player. When "Bernadette" started, it blew my mind. I *had* to know how to play that song, no matter how long it took me.

How To Play It

"Bernadette" is no walk in the park. It's technically very demanding, and you'll need all the skills you've mastered to make this sound great. You must be adept at rapid-fire arpeggios and complicated funk rhythms. If you want to sound credible playing "Bernadette," you must also be comfortable playing in a demanding key like E♭. The good news is you can do it. If you've faithfully studied the bass and worked on your arpeggios enough, you're ready to tackle one of the baddest bass tunes of all time.

I once spoke to the great Bob Babbitt (bassist on "Cool Jerk" and "Signed Sealed, Delivered, I'm Yours") about the classic Motown tunes being in flat keys. He told me the writers found it easier to compose in flat keys (just hit the black keys on a piano!), but, more importantly, they felt those keys *sounded* better. And they were right; E♭ is a bright sounding key. "Bernadette" really catches your ear in the key of E♭. It might not have the same impact in E or D.

The notation is clear-cut. Tablature and measure subdivision will show you what to play and where to play it on the fretboard. Jamerson's subtlety and nuance is very difficult to uncover even for a seasoned transcriber, but the exact bass part is notated for you here. There's

a lot going on, and you'll need to practice this song very slowly to get the feel of the arpeggios during the chorus (starting at measure 3). Pay close attention to the routine in beats 3–4 of measure 6: D♭–E♭–A♭–**low** B♭–D♭–D–E♭. This lick has been misquoted consistently over the years. When you lock in with the recording, this lick will feel amazing.

The verse can be tricky. Pay particular attention to measure 13 (beats 3–4), as this is another important lick to nail. It may seem that the notes here come from left field (especially the open E), but they truly sound incredible in context. It's a terrific lick and nicely sums up the essence of Jamerson's style—*never* generic. Jamerson could be crafty. He knew how to be melodic and interesting by avoiding the diatonically *correct* notes at clever moments. As tough as these parts appear, you'll find they are very playable because they come from deep within the groove.

Vital Stats

Bassist: James Jamerson

Song: "Bernadette"

Album: *Reach Out –*
The Four Tops, 1967

Age at time of recording: 24

Bass: 1962 Fender Precision Bass

Amp: Recorded direct into the console

Bernadette

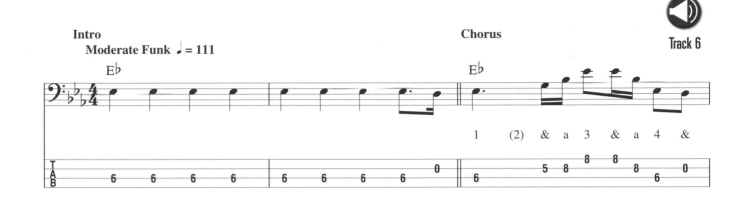

Tommy Cogbill

"Respect" gets respect. Released in 1967, Aretha Franklin's rendition of the Otis Redding penned song is the definitive version. Everything is right about this song: sung by the Queen of Soul, the bass part almost steals the show, the horns are stunningly arranged, and the background vocals are gospel cool.

Producer Jerry Wexler originally came across Otis Redding's song and brought it to Aretha's attention. Redding's version was popular among his core R&B audience, but Jerry felt the song had potential to be a crossover hit. Aretha's "Respect" was much more successful and spent two weeks atop the Billboard Pop Singles chart. It also became an international hit, reaching #10 in the United Kingdom. Even Otis Redding was impressed and was quoted affectionately describing "Respect" as "the song that little girl done stole from me."

Aretha Franklin was born in 1942. Known for her soul recordings, she was also fluent in jazz, rock, blues, pop, R&B, and gospel. In 2008, *Rolling Stone* magazine ranked her #1 on its list of Greatest Singers of All Time. She won 20 Grammies and has had 45 Top 40 hits to her credit. In 1987, Aretha became the first female artist to be inducted into the Rock and Roll Hall of Fame.

Tommy Cogbill (see also "Mustang Sally") was a Tennessee boy, born in 1932. He was a member of the famed Muscle Shoals rhythm section but was also in demand in Nashville. An acclaimed be-bop guitarist prior to taking up the bass, he's one of the few players who was able to use his knowledge on guitar, transfer it to bass, and make it believable. His dynamic interpretation on bass was uncanny, and his sense of time was amazing. Mike Leech notes, "After a cut, when he had played something outstanding (such as the bass line on 'Memphis Soul Stew') and compliments were paid, he never claimed all the credit. He always passed credit around, usually by saying something like, 'pretty funky groove, huh?'"

Top Nashville session bassist Michael Rhodes said of Tommy Cogbill, "There are plenty of correlations between James Jamerson and Tommy Cogbill, including their jazz backgrounds and their parallel careers. Like James, Tommy was a take-charge guy in the studio; he would stand up and count off the songs and basically run the session. He had such a strong presence in the music he played that there was a

© Photofest

Aretha Franklin

> *"Tommy Cogbill's profile has always been subdued—as he wanted it to be. However, from a historical perspective, he should be listed among the top five most important popular music bassists of the last century."*
> —Mike Leech, bassist for Elvis Presley

sort of natural deference by the rest of the band."

Tommy is still relatively unknown by name, although not by his bass lines. His trademark busy-yet-unimposing parts can be heard on Wilson Pickett's "Funky Broadway," Elvis Presley's "Kentucky Rain" and "In the Ghetto," the Box Tops' "Cry Like a Baby," Aretha Franklin's "(You Make Me Feel Like a) Natural Woman," "Chain of Fools," and Dusty Springfield's "Son of a Preacher Man."

Michael Rhodes said, "Tommy taught me everything from studio demeanor to the role of the bass player. He innately knew how to approach a track and make it work. He was a soft-spoken, laid-back guy, but with a bass in his hands, he had the intuitive ability to create forward motion through a song that enabled everyone else to surf in the wake." Mike Leech adds, "Tommy's playing was always headed toward something—the next chord change or the next section. In retrospect, his playing was heading toward the future of electric bass."

Tommy eventually added producing to his skills, most notably behind the board for Neil Diamond's monster hit, "Sweet Caroline." On December 7, 1982, at age 50, he succumbed to a stroke, and the music world lost one of its greatest contributors.

How to Play It

Part of the allure of "Respect" came from the bass pulsing through the speakers of a 1960s tube car radio. It was undeniable—an old Fender bass was used with flatwound strings. However, it wasn't old then; it was brand new. But little has been done over the years to improve the tone of a bass. Back in the early days, the chrome bridge cover was usually left on the bass, and for good reason. There was a piece of foam glued to the roof of the bridge cover. When placed over the strings, it acted as a mute, which increased the percussiveness of

Otis Redding wrote this and originally recorded it in 1965. His version consisted of only verses, no chorus or bridge. It was Aretha's idea to cover this song. She came up with the arrangement and added the "sock it to me" lines.

the bass. That was all part of the classic Fender bass tone. Years later, bassists would buy Fenders in hopes of getting that sound. But the newer ones came without chrome cover plates and hence no string mutes. Additionally, modern basses were being strung with round wound strings, as opposed to flatwound. While this increased sustain and was good for rock 'n' roll songs and slapping, it was not so good if you wanted that classic, warm, punchy R&B thang.

"Respect" is a must-learn for all aspiring groove masters. The tune is in the key of C and is full of dominant 7th chords. Interestingly, however, the bass line doesn't hit many 7ths. It's more concerned with 6ths, which are typical of supporting simple major chords. But that's a big part of the bass line's allure; it's not too literal. The 6ths come close enough to the dominants to just tickle the harmonic structure—and it works. Typically, you couldn't get away with this if they were minor chords. You'd normally have to substitute the minor 7th for the 6th, although there are some notable exceptions (such as Jamerson's stellar line on the Four Tops' "I Can't Help Myself").

The tune opens on the chorus groove. The first thing to notice is the rhythmic contrast between measures. Measure 1 bounces steadily between eighth and sixteenth notes, firmly accenting each beat, but measure 2 answers with constant, syncopated eighths. Consequently, this two-measure phrase breathes and continually propels the song forward. The verse is treated to the same alternating rhythmic treatment.

Clearly, the bass opts for major 6ths to create its routine during the verse and chorus, as discussed above. But Cogbill does acknowledge the dominant 7th chord

during the transition from verse to chorus. Here, he plays the ♭7th (E♭) when it descends scale-wise from F7 to the C7.

In contrast to the verse and chorus, the bridge straightens out the chordal and scalar structure, as it opts for roots and 5ths. However, notice that it's still quite busy rhythmically with eighths and sixteenths. This keeps it from dragging as the key shifts from C major to E major. The F♯m7–B7 chord progression is a ii–V cadence in E, though the E chord is never sounded. The key returns to C when G7 is introduced in measure 21 to round out the section. Typically, a bridge is a study in contrast from the rest of the tune, and this tune is an excellent example.

If you listen closely to the original recording, you'll hear the guitar is barely audible as it doubles the bass line. During the verse, the guitar drops out, and the bass is left alone to drive the groove. The verse seems more haunting as a result. Most people don't consciously notice this, but they'd probably miss it if things were different. To put it another way: the listener responds on a subconscious level, aesthetically feeling the change in mood. The chorus, as a result, has more edge when the guitar doubles the bass line.

Vital Stats

Bassist: Tommy Cogbill

Song: "Respect"

Album: *I Never Loved a Man the Way I Love You* – Aretha Franklin, 1967

Age at time of recording: 35

Bass: Early '60s Fender Precision Bass

Amp: 1960s piggyback Fender Bassman amp mixed with a direct feed into the mixing console

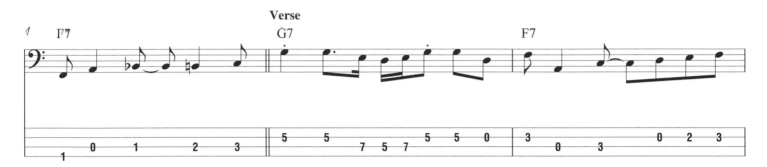

Words and Music by Otis Redding

Donald "Duck" Dunn

© Getty

"A lot of people thought Duck Dunn was a black guy. We got the soul sound by blending our country and blues influences. I grew up with the Grand Ole Opry. When we mixed that feel with the blues, we got something new."

—Donald "Duck" Dunn

on *Saturday Night Live* in the seventies and again in the movie *The Blues Brothers*. Today, "Soul Man" can be heard being played by just about any band in any bar in any city in the USA.

As a member of Stax Records house band, Booker T. & the MG's, Donald "Duck" Dunn helped create one of pop music's most enduring legacies—the sound of Memphis soul: a sly co-mingling of country & western shuffle and lazy blues, with a dramatic dash of gospel tossed in to keep up the heat. They recorded hit after hit for Wilson Pickett, Otis Redding, Albert King, and many others.

"Soul Man" (Atlantic Records), written by Isaac Hayes and David Porter, was a very successful hit for soul duo Sam & Dave. Isaac found the inspiration for "Soul Man" in the turmoil of the sixties civil rights movement. He noticed black Detroit residents had marked the buildings that had not been destroyed with the word "soul." Isaac and David came up with the idea of (in Isaac's words) "a story about one's struggle to rise above his present conditions. It's almost a tune where it's kind of like boasting 'I'm a soul man.' It's a pride thing."

The idea worked big time, and Sam & Dave's "Soul Man" was the most successful Stax single to date upon its release. The single peaked at #2 on the Hot 100 in the USA and received a Grammy in 1968. It was revived when the Blues Brothers (Dan Akroyd and John Belushi) performed the song

Donald "Duck" Dunn was born on November 24, 1941 (died May 13, 2012), in Memphis, Tennessee. Nicknamed "Duck" for watching Donald Duck cartoons with his father, he was a childhood friend of guitarist Steve Cropper (also a member of the MG's). Steve noted how self-taught Duck started out playing along with records, filling in what he thought should be there. "That's why Duck Dunn's bass lines are very unique." He added, "They're not locked into somebody's schoolbook somewhere." Booker T. & the MG's was founded by Steve and Booker T. Jones in 1962. The original bassist, heard on early hits such as "Green Onions," was Lewie Steinberg, but Duck replaced him in 1965.

Interestingly, Duck did not care for the Stax recording room. "I thought we sounded terrible in that room—I hated it. They were always asking me to play with a lot of highs, and it just sounded too trebly to me. But we'd walk out and

listen to the playback, and the bass would sound round as could be. I couldn't hear it when we were playing, but somehow our sound always made it to tape."

Duck also had a similar attitude about live gigs (as most bassists, including yours truly, experienced). "When I'm onstage, I hate what I call the 'roomful of boom,' where the low end is just roaring. I've found that if you use a lot of highs onstage, the sound rounds off—just like it did at Stax."

Along with the Funk Brothers in Motown, the MG's were among the first racially integrated R&B bands. Duck remembered, "A lot of people thought I was a pick-up bass player; they thought Duck Dunn was a black guy who couldn't make the tour for some reason. In Europe, they'd ask me, 'What's it like to play with a black man?' I never knew what to say. We didn't think that way; we just played."

The MG's drummer was the powerful Al Jackson, Jr., and Duck loved working with him. "Al just had that groove—that big pocket with the delayed feel. If there's any secret to my playing, I think it comes from what Al used to tell me: 'Just wait on two.' With him, it could be an awfully long wait. He had an amazing sense of time, and he knew how to shape a song. A lot of what he did sounds so simple, but nobody else could play that way. Every band has its disagreements about how a song should go, but it became clear that when Al came up with something, it was going to end up being perfect for the song. And like I always say, if the drums and bass ain't happening, nothing's happening."

After the MG's, Duck Dunn went on to play for Muddy Waters, Freddie King, Jerry Lee Lewis, Eric Clapton, and many more. He got to display his quirky Southern humor while making the two *Blues Brothers* movies. One of his lines was, "We had a band that could turn goat piss into gasoline!"

In June 2004, Duck, Steve, and Booker served as the house band for Eric Clapton's Crossroads Guitar Festival. The group backed all the living blues guitar legends on the main stage at the Cotton

Producer Isaac Hayes wanted the record to have rhythmic elements similar to Bo Diddley's song "Bo Diddley," and co-producer David Porter asked singer Sam Moore to give him "the Bobby Bland squall."

Bowl in Dallas, Texas. Duck performed occasionally with Booker T. & the MG's at music festivals and nightclubs until his death. In 2007, the MG's received a Lifetime Achievement Grammy for their contributions to pop music.

Sam & Dave were Sam Moore and Dave Prater. Moore was in the Melionaires Gospel group, and Prater was a solo artist before they met in 1961. They were signed by Roulette in 1962 and switched to Atlantic in 1965 before recording for Stax. In 1988, Prater was killed in a car crash. They were inducted into the Rock and Roll Hall of Fame in 1992. Some of their biggest hits included "I Thank You" and "Hold On, I'm Comin'," but "Soul Man" was by far their shining moment at the top of the pops.

How to Play It

The bass to "Soul Man" is the soul of the tune. It plays counter to the rhythm guitar but outlines the chords about as fluently as can be done. Duck always had a knack for hitting the nail right on the head when it came to picking just the right bass part. You might be able to find a convenient way to play this tune with some crafty use of open strings, but, it's not likely the bass line was approached this way. The proof would be the modulation after the bridge. From that point on, you're stuck in a fretted position to pull off the routine in Ab. Logically, the main body of the song was probably approached with the same fingering pattern.

This signature riff can probably be accomplished with a shift to the C on the A string, but you might end up with a bit more string noise than you would like. Consequently, I've noted in

the transcription the most economical fretting position as well as fret-hand fingering. What makes this four-fret stretch preferred is the rake down to C on the E string. This deepens the groove; the rake *always* deepens the groove. It is often said the best technique is when it is not noticed at all. The rake makes your "technique" almost undetectable. The listener just hears *music*, which is all we ever want.

Notice the deliberate contrast between chorus and verse. The bass is very active through the verse, mixing syncopated eighth and sixteenth notes. In the chorus, static pedaling eighth-note roots drive the groove. This makes the bass line feel balanced and symmetrical. This strategy can only help the overall song and its impact on the listener.

The bridge is most interesting, as the key changes from G to Eb. Be ready for this! At its conclusion, the section makes more sense, as we again modulate from the Eb to Ab. Ultimately, this lifts the original verse key up a half step (G to Ab). Again, work on your shifting so nobody notices your technique as you navigate through the verse groove. Play slowly at first, and then slowly increase the speed until you can comfortably play at the final tempo. All bassists with soul *love* to play "Soul Man."

Vital Stats

Bassist: Donald "Duck" Dunn

Song: "Soul Man"

Album: *Soul Men* – Sam & Dave, 1967

Age at time of recording: 26

Bass: 1957 Fender Precision Bass

Amp: Ampeg B-15 amp mixed with a direct feed into the console

Track 8

Intro
Moderate Funk ♩ = 112

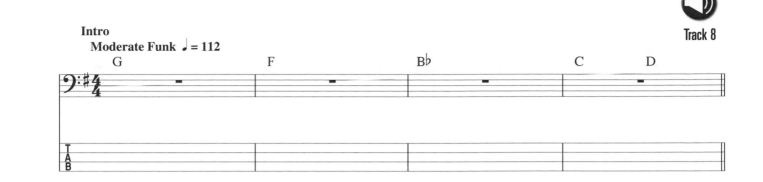

Verse

Chorus

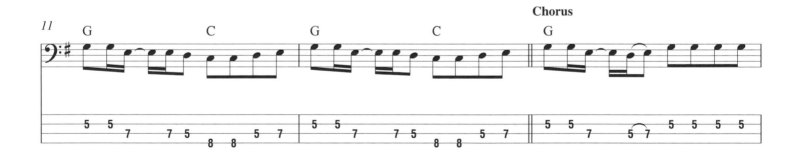

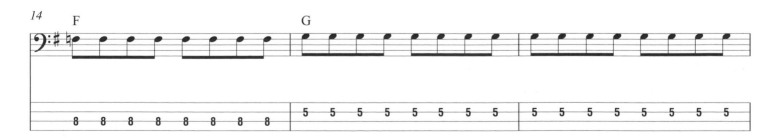

Words and Music by Isaac Hayes and David Porter
Copyright © 1967 ALMO MUSIC CORP. and WALDEN MUSIC, INC.
Copyright Renewed
All Rights Reserved   Used by Permission

Jack Bruce

"If you're talking about the best electric bass players, it's very, very simple: James Jamerson, Paul McCartney, Jaco Pastorius, me."
—Jack Bruce

© Photofest

The British rock group Cream, consisting of bassist Jack Bruce, guitarist Eric Clapton, and drummer Ginger Baker, is retrospectively considered the first supergroup. Jack's powerful singing and bass playing lie at the nucleus of their sound. Though their career lasted only a few years, they were very successful, having sold in excess of 35 million albums worldwide. Bruce was also the main songwriter, having penned their biggest hit, "Sunshine of Your Love," with lyricist Peter Brown. The opening riff is instantly recognizable to nearly anyone and everyone.

In May of 1967, after a brief tour of the USA, Cream entered Atlantic Studios in New York City to record their legendary second album, *Disraeli Gears*. With little time left on their visitors visa, they had

no time to spare. Urban legend claims the album was recorded in just three days. In fact, the sessions spanned from May 8–19. Felix Pappalardi produced, and Tom Dowd engineered the sessions. Tom was amazed at the amount of gear they brought. "They were incredible. They recorded at ear shattering levels. I never saw anything so powerful in my life, and it was just frightening. I don't think they were cognizant of the fact that

they had more tracks. They just went about recording in their own method."

Pappalardi was a perfect fit for Cream, and Dowd was considered a premier engineer of the time (and, as history has shown, of all time). But Ahmet Ertegun, president of Atlantic Records, didn't understand what the group was about. Ertegun thought of Cream as Eric's band. He decided Jack and Ginger were backup musicians. Both clearly sensed this, and Jack was particularly miffed, as he was the songwriter and main vocalist of the band. In spite of this dynamic, they were able to create a legendary album.

Jack was particularly bothered by the attitude towards his songs. He stated, "I came up with things like 'Sunshine of Your Love' and 'White Room,' and Ertegun would say 'No, that's no good; it's psychedelic hogwash, and, anyway you shouldn't be singing. Eric has to be the lead singer. You're just the bass player.'" By virtue of the fact that the band didn't have enough material to fill an album, the studio had to record "Sunshine of Your Love," which, ironically, went on to become the biggest selling single that Atlantic had ever had!

Co-writer Pete Brown explained how the song came about. "Jack and I had been up all night, trying to get something together, and it hadn't been going well. In desperation, he picked up his string

bass and said, 'Well, what about this?', and played this riff, and I said 'Wait a minute' and looked outside—'it's getting near dawn, when lights close their tired eyes'... and that's absolutely how it happened. It was five o'clock in the morning, the birds were twittering, and we were feeling terrible."

To this day, musicians and non-musicians marvel at the album *Disreali Gears*. It has truly stood the test of time. Every student who enters my studio always wants to know how to play "Sunshine of Your Love."

Jack Bruce became a bass god during the reign of Cream. He, Ginger Baker, and Eric Clapton would furiously improvise extended renditions of their classic tracks. There has never been another band like them, to this day. He kept going strong, recording and touring with British guitar legend Robin Trower throughout Europe, until his death in 2014.

Clapton got the idea for the album title after a roadie told him about the derailleur gears on his bicycle. Derailleur, pronounced "di-rail-yer," is the kind of gear commonly found on 10-speed bikes. The roadie mispronounced it "disraeli," which led to the classic title.

How to Play It

The main riff of the song *is* the blues scale. It is arguably the most used (and overused) scale in all of rock music. Used with taste, it is one of the most *usable* scales of all. The intervals consist of root, minor 3rd, perfect 4th, augmented 4th, perfect 5th, and minor 7th. As "Sunshine of Your Love" is in the key of D, the notes of the scale are D–F–G–G♯–A–C.

There is only one place on the fretboard to play this song correctly. Start in fifth position exactly as Jack Bruce played,

with your first finger on the fifth fret. The first note (D) is played with either the pinky or ring finger. Refer to the notation and tablature for proper notes and fingering positions. The song follows the typical I–IV chord progression (D to G), seeming to progress like a 12-bar blues. However, at the arrival of the V chord (A), the riff gives way to a two-measure chord sequence consisting of A–C–G that creates the chorus. The bass sticks to roots here, which contrasts the verse and creates a sense of balance. Good taste and musical sensibility go hand in hand with creativity. They also make for great and successful song crafting.

It's one thing to be able to navigate this bass line without mistakes. It's another to play it in perfect time, with a punchy and articulate tone, and convey a sense of *attitude*. You *live* the song while you play. Feel and draw from the energy that emanates from your musical soul. You must play this song with a great sense of conviction.

Vital Stats

Bassist: Jack Bruce

Song: "Sunshine of Your Love"

Album: *Disraeli Gears* – Cream, 1967

Age at time of recording: 25

Bass: '60s Gibson EB-3

Amp: Marshall Super Bass 100 valve amp with Marshal 4x12 cabinet

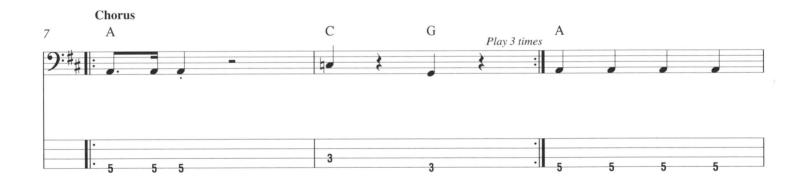

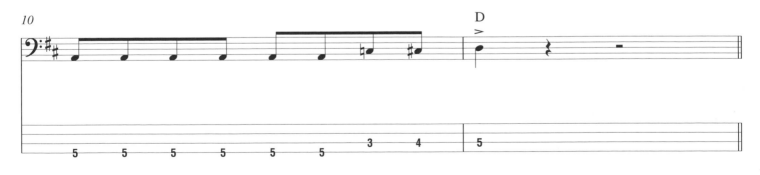

James Jamerson

"'For Once in My Life' is phenomenal. That's a concerto for bass. He used to do things that sounded like he was going lower than E—and I thought that he tuned down—but he didn't. There is no bassist in R&B that changed the concept of commercial music like James Jamerson."

—Gene Page, Motown arranger

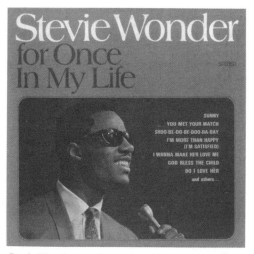

Stevie Wonder was born six weeks premature and developed retrolental fibroplasia, now technically known as retinopathy of prematurity, which caused his blindness. Stevie says he tries to create "sonic pictures" with his songs.

"For Once in My Life" is a song written by Ron Miller and Orlando Murden for Motown's Jobete publishing company in 1967. Jean DuShon originally recorded the composition, and other artists like Tony Bennett and the Temptations have recorded slow ballad renditions of the song. The most familiar and successful version is this up-tempo hit by Stevie Wonder, which was recorded immediately after DuShon's original. Wonder's version, issued on Motown's Tamla label in 1968, hit #2 on the Billboard Pop Singles and R&B Singles charts. "For Once in My Life" is an absolute tour de force for the bass. James is at the top of his game, and for many Jamerson-philes, this song is one of his best recordings.

Stevie Wonder was born Stevland Hardaway Judkins on May 13, 1950. His name was later changed to Stevland Hardaway Morris. Blind since birth, Stevie started playing piano at seven, mastering the instrument by nine. A year later, by age ten, he'd mastered drums and harmonica. He also learned how to play bass in those early years. In 1961, at the age of eleven, Stevie was discovered singing on a street corner by a relative of one of the Miracles, who introduced him to the CEO of Motown. He was signed to Motown's Tamla label as Little Stevie Wonder. At thirteen, he enjoyed a huge hit with "Fingertips (Pt. 2)," a live version featuring Little Stevie Wonder on vocals, harmonica, and bongos. (Coincidentally, his drummer at the time was a very young Marvin Gaye.)

Soon, Stevie dropped the "Little" from his stage name and continued to have incredible success as a recording artist throughout the sixties. In the early seventies, he gained complete artistic control over his music and released *Music of My Mind* (1972), the live *Talking Book* (1972), *Innervisions* (1973), and *Songs in the Key of Life* (1976). He sang and played all the instruments on his studio recordings from this period. Highly acclaimed both critically and commercially, these albums propelled him to superstar status.

"For Once in My Life" is yet another bit of recording history displaying Jamerson's genius (see also "Bernadette," "Roadrunner," and "What's Going On"). James was so revered by his fellow studio musicians that a track was only considered a "keeper" if he got up from his stool at the end of a take. No words were spoken, but all eyes were always on James as a song ended. If he got up, that was the one; if he remained seated, they were not done.

How to Play It

This is one of the more advanced bass lines in this book. In fact, it might be the toughest of all. The great James Jamerson *makes* the tune with his inventive and relentless lines. To this day, it remains one of the most demanding bass lines to play. Beyond its technical difficulty, it's also brilliant for its musicality alone. The chords are moving every two beats, but the bass never sounds as if it's "chasing the chords." Rather, it sounds like playing "through the chords," much like an accomplished soloist would.

The bass player should not always feel compelled to outline all the defining tones of each chord. Rather, if you concern yourself with propelling the song forward with tasteful rhythm and a "passing wink" at the individual chord

details, the bass line will seemingly have more vision.

Specifically, notice that the bass line doesn't incorporate the augmented interval (♯5th) for the F+ chord. Not until the F♯° in measure 8 does the bass actually arppegiate the chord. As a result, the bass line "breathes" in measure 7 and delivers the chordal details in measure 2. This approach keeps the bass line from becoming too literal. You have to know when this approach works and, more importantly, when it won't. Studying and mastering this tune will aid you in acquiring the musical wisdom of knowing when to push (and when not to push) the harmonic envelope.

Make sure you practice this song very slowly so you can gain control of your instrument. If you pay close attention to the notation subdivision, the rhythm will be obvious. This time, I purposely subdivided only when notes are played. Downbeats are left out if nothing is played on them. Rhythmic subdivision is often done this way, so you should become familiar with this method. Tap your foot and try sounding out the rhythms like in measure 7: "1 + … a 3…a 4 e +." The more you do this, the easier it gets.

Refer to the tablature, because the first position (first finger on fret 1) is essential in making this tune feel right. Consider putting flatwound (or tapewound) strings on your bass, and maybe slide a piece of foam rubber under your strings near the bridge. This will make your bass punchier and cut down on sustain. It will also give you more control over the open strings. Getting control of open strings (with or without the help of foam) is crucial. In fact, you should ideally practice with and without foam under your strings. Additionally, your fretting hand needs to "lay down" on the strings

to dampen them. This will come after logging hours and hours of practice. Be patient, and remember that Rome wasn't built in a day.

Similarly, your plucking hand needs to utilize unused fingers to help mute vibrating strings. Your thumb should rest on the E string when you play the D or G strings to avoid any sympathetic vibration. Similarly, your pinky should rest on the A string when you strike A on the G string. You must listen for unintended vibration from any and all strings and eliminate it. Later, when you reinsert the foam piece under your strings, your performance will sound amazing!

You'll know you've mastered this tune because your fretting hand will comfortably remain in first position. Your plucking hand will also be efficiently silencing string vibration while simultaneously digging into the groove. The illusion will be created that you aren't working very hard to play this song; it will feel as though the bass is playing itself. People watching will be blown away, because they'll hear this amazing music coming out of your bass, but it will look effortless. That is exactly what you want to convey when performing.

Vital Stats

Bassist: James Jamerson

Song: "For Once in My Life"

Album: *For Once in My Life* – Stevie Wonder, 1968

Age at time of recording: 31

Bass: 1962 Fender Precision Bass ("The Funk Machine")

Amp: Recorded direct into the console (Ampeg B-15 was used as a monitor in the studio)

For Once in My Life

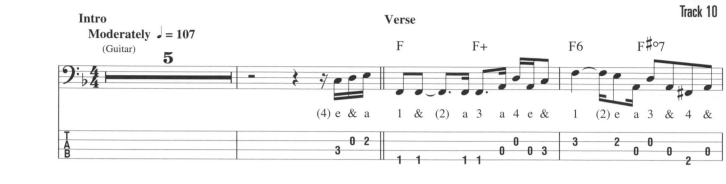

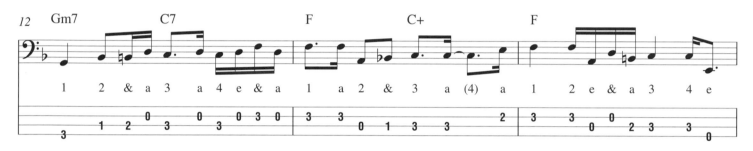

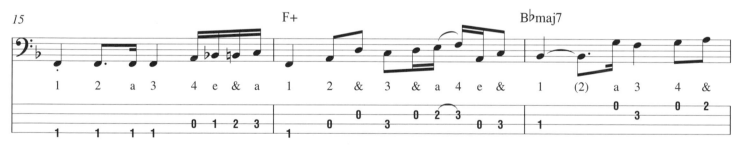

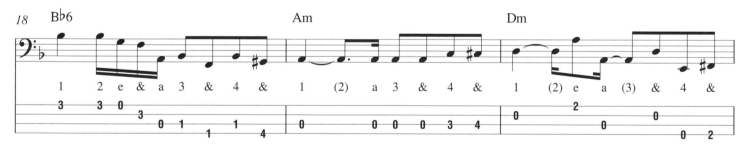

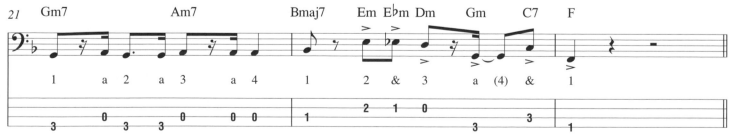

Words by Ronald Miller
Music by Orlando Murden

George Porter, Jr.

"May your groove be phat"
—George Porter, Jr.

© Getty

"Cissy Strut" was recorded and released by the Meters in 1969. An instrumental tune in the style of New Orleans funk, it's become a staple of cover bands everywhere. Sax players, guitar players, and even drummers *love* to jam endlessly on "Cissy Strut." The bass player gets to "solo" with a "phat" groove underneath those other more self-indulgent solos.

The bassist wins the solo contest because he holds it all together with a "loosey goosey" simple, spontaneous-sounding pocket between a V (G7) and a I (C) chord. The trick is to keep it all moving forward without overplaying. A simple bass groove will get the job done every time, no matter how long the others want to keep soloing. A redundant bass line is boring and is not the way to approach a "Cissy Strut" extended jam. You can play a sparse, syncopated pocket that continually evolves with subtle nuance. If approached artistically, neither you nor the listener should ever get bored.

The Meters, an American funk band from New Orleans, Louisiana, performed and recorded from the late sixties until 1977 and played an influential role as backing musicians for other artists like Dr. John and Lee Dorsey. They never achieved mainstream commercial success, but they were significant as progenitors of funk, influencing both their contemporaries and musicians after their heyday.

Formed in 1965, the band featured vocalist Art Neville, guitarist Leo Nocentelli, bassist George Porter, Jr., drummer Ziggy Modeliste, and percussionist Cyril Neville. They became the house band for Allen Toussaint and his record label, Sansu Enterprises. They changed labels in 1972 and, unfortunately, had a hard time getting back on the charts. However, their reputation preceded them. They played on many important albums for people such as Paul McCartney, Labelle, and Robert Palmer. The Rolling Stones invited the Meters to open for them on their Tour of America in 1975.

New Orleans has produced more than its share of funky bass kings. But to countless players in the Crescent City and beyond, George Porter, Jr. reigns supreme. George talks about the influence of early R&B records and the lack of bass: "You can't hear the bass or the kick drum at all; it's all piano, vocals, and guitars. A lot of it was played with acoustic bass that wasn't recorded too well; that made me want the bass to be punchier when I recorded with the Meters. I started off thinking there had to be lots of bottom, but with the little bitty stereo speakers most people have, it's not bottom you want, but punch. You want to get to the point where you can hear the note, and then you add maybe 2dB of bass, just to round out the notes."

George is not a fan of the roundwound twang of today's bassists: "I like strings that are old and dull. My strings leave the bass when they break. I would never, ever play a bass that has all brand-new strings on it; if I have to change all four of my strings, the bass is gonna sit around a while before I play on it."

When asked about New Orleans funk and the role of the bass and drums,

The Meters just might be the most under-appreciated act in funk, because most of their music over the years didn't feature vocals. You probably don't know "Cissy Strut" by name, but if you listen to the instrumental, it's likely that you've heard at it one point in time.

George said, "Bass players and drummers from New Orleans play more together than guys from anywhere else. In music from other places, there's a tendency for the bass player to play right after the kick drum. In New Orleans, they're more closely linked, playing in sync almost all the time. The bass might venture away from the kick drum to play more notes, but at some point—maybe two and four—we always meet."

About drummer Zigaboo, George elaborates: "Zig and I created the bottom that everything grew on, and I think what Zig did on drums is undeniably the funkiest shit on the planet. But what he did, for some reason or another, has not made it to this time period. The drummers today do not have those tools in their toolbox."

George comments about how the Meters put a song together: "Zig would start a groove and Leo would be the second guy in. It usually took me a few minutes to figure out what the hell Zig was doing. I'd be sitting there listening and watching to make sure I had the same one that he had, because a lot of stuff he played could be interpreted differently. He used to throw off Art with some of those grooves. Art would say, 'Where's one?' Where you come in can change the whole concept of where one is. It was all intuitive—we definitely didn't write out charts or anything like that."

As to the state of funk today, George is not too happy: "I don't know what is considered funk today. Funk music today is hip-hop, I guess. Syncopation is out. Syncopation is history. In my dealings with people at record companies, I keep being told that my music ain't funky. They say it's too syncopated. People have to think about how to dance to music when it's syncopated, because it's not just straight 4/4. Syncopation is like jazz—it wasn't meant for the masses, just a hip few."

How to Play It

This song is not very difficult to execute, but the groove is another classic, and the feel is real. There's a quarter-step bend that adds to the feel, so it must be mastered in your quest for R&B proficiency. Think *light swing*; this tune is *not* straight sixteenths, but it's not full swing either. Just lean slightly toward a swing feel, and you'll have it.

The main riff is a Cm7 arpeggio (descending from the octave). Refer to the tablature for the most natural choices for note location. The E♭ is treated to the quarter-step bend to access the true blue note that lies in between a minor and major 3rd. This is answered with a walk up: G–A–C. This is another often misquoted lick. Many people often play B♭ instead of A, which isn't near as hip.

The bass concludes the main riff with a high 5th (G) to low 5th (G) rake. This is accomplished with one finger of the plucking hand. Pluck the high G on the D string, rake through the A string, making sure your fret-hand fingers are muting the A string completely, and finish the rake with a low 5th (G) on the E string. This rake is all about percussion, rhythm, and harmony. Percussion is created with the rake of the dead A string. Rhythm comes from the swinging sixteenth notes through the rake, along with the eighth-note pickup note (C) that precedes the rake. And harmony is created

when the bass emphasizes the low 5th (G) at the end.

The B section is a straight-ahead box pattern based on the root, 5th, ♭7th, and octave three-fret box. Keep your fret-hand fingers close together like a bunch of bananas here. Just be sure you don't get confused and play 7ths instead of 5ths, or vice versa.

The solo sections vamp on C. Here the bass groove is wide and deep. It doesn't have to be complicated, but it does have to be solid. It's just roots (C), high and low 5ths (G), and low 3rds (open E). In measure 7, the major 7th (B) leading tone precedes the tonic (C) for emphasis. Steady as she goes here. When you're forced to play only chord tones (and an occasional leading tone) for your solo accompaniment, you can truly discover what pocket playing is all about. The groove is the only thing that matters. Let your "bunch of bananas" lay down on those strings as your plucking hand strokes them for rhythmic texture. Don't rush your part. Lay that groove like it's a hot muggy night in N'Orlins.

Vital Stats

Bassist: George Porter, Jr.

Song: "Cissy Strut"

Album: *The Meters –* The Meters, 1969

Age at time of recording: 22

Bass: Melody Plus bass

Amp: Fender Bassman 50 with 2x12 cabinet

By Arthur Neville, Leo Nocentelli, George Porter and Joseph Modeliste, Jr.
© 1969 (Renewed 1997) SCREEN GEMS-EMI MUSIC INC.

Andy Fraser

"All Right Now" put the English rock band Free on the international musical map. Released in the summer of 1970, it shot to #4 on the US singles charts. Written by bassist Andy Fraser in the University of Durham student union building after a show, the song originally appeared on the *Fire and Water* album (Island Records), which was produced by Chris Blackwell.

I spoke with Andy about how he came up with the idea for the song. "'All Right Now' was initiated after one of Free's most miserable gigs. A rainy Tuesday, in a very forgettable town, and there were only about 30 people there. All of them whacked out on Mandrax—a downer that was very popular in those days—bumping into each other, which today would kinda look like a slow-motion mosh-pit. They basically ignored us, which was OK; we were usually very content to play for ourselves. But... we sucked."

"In the dressing room afterwards, there was this terrible silence—like the world had come to an end, and in attempt to lighten the vibe, I began singing 'All Right Now'—sort of like a parent to a sulking child, with a little edge in there like 'don't be such a baby.' Hence the beginning of a new three-chord trick."

Andy continued about the actual recording of the song: "The album was first recorded at Trident studios, with one of their house engineers Roy Thomas Baker. Island's Chris Blackwell wanted to remix it, edit it, add some overdubs, at Island's new studios, and we wanted Roy to complete it with us, though he was deadly nervous about Trident finding out he was working outside their studio. So we had to sneak him in, dead of night, and he completed sessions in a complete sweat because of his concerns. He even refused to be credited on album, for the same reason. Strange story."

Countless bands have covered the song. Even Steve Miller admitted that his guitar intro to "Rock 'N Me" was a direct rip of the "All Right Now'" intro. The opening guitar line hooked you at the get-go, and the vocal took you by the throat. After the breakdown, the bass tied you up and just would not let go until the guitar solo was over. You didn't know whether to follow the bass or follow the guitar solo. Both were irresistible.

Free was formed in 1968 in London, England and featured lead singer Paul Rodgers, drummer Simon Kirke, lead guitarist Paul Kossoff, and bassist Andy Fraser. The band was known for its incredible live shows and continuous

One of the engineers on the original recording was Roy Thomas Baker, who later gained fame as producer for Queen. Free's lead singer, Paul Rodgers, later toured with Queen as their lead singer, after the passing of Freddie Mercury.

> *"One couldn't ask for more than playing with the likes of Rodgers, Kossoff, and Kirke—total masters in their field. Our confidence came from our total belief in each other."*
> —Free bassist Andy Fraser

touring. Early studio albums did not sell very well, but that all changed with *Fire and Water*. This album transformed them to one of the top rock bands of the seventies. The song in particular helped secure them a place at the huge Isle of Wight Festival in 1970, at which they performed for 600,000.

Most remarkable about Free was how young they all were when the band formed: Andy was 15, Paul Kossoff was 17, and Simon and Paul Rodgers were both 18. Also remarkable was the fact that, after their huge success with 1970's *Fire and Water*, they had broken up by 1972. Simon Kirke and Paul Rodgers went on to form Bad Company, Andy formed the Sharks (and later the Andy Fraser Band), and Kossoff formed Backstreet Crawler.

Andy spoke fondly when remembering Free. "It was like a team of commandos where you knew we were all watching each other's back. We were sensitive to each other's weaknesses and had the chemistry to always be able to fill in the gaps, pick up the slack—complete the whole. A real band/marriage in every sense."

In April 2006, Fraser responded to the revival of interest in his music by announcing two rare live shows at the Temecula Community Arts Theatre in Temecula, California on May 4. Highlighted by an eight-piece band, this was his first live performance since the Woodstock 1994 reunion with Paul Rodgers. In 2008, Fraser wrote and sang the song "Obama (Yes We Can)" in support of Barack Obama's presidential campaign.

Andy was known for a very unique style of playing during his Free years. He had a percussive and non-linear style of playing. Many of his routines had a very staccato feel, and even though he didn't use an envelope filter such as a Mu-Tron or Q-Tron, his bass had an unusual "bark"—sounding at times almost tuba-esque.

How to Play It

Because he is physically a smaller man, Andy found the Gibson EB-3 to be the perfect size bass to play—the same model that Jack Bruce made famous with Cream (see "Sunshine of Your Love"). That particular bass is renowned for its short scale neck but also its special tone due to the bridge pickup. This bridge pickup enhances that percussive "bark" for which Andy was known. When you attempt to play the bass line during the guitar solo of "All Right Now," in which you're constantly jumping back and forth two octaves at a time, it'll become apparent to you that a short scale bass would be just the right call. Andy Fraser knew exactly what he was doing.

The verse is easy enough to execute, but the *thought* behind the part is brilliant. First of all, you have to be confident in playing short staccato notes with *space* between each note. One might try to fill the space in with either longer notes or more notes. That strategy exposes an inherent lack of confidence in one's bass playing. Andy's strategy on the chorus is a classic example of "it's not what you play, it's what you *don't* play that counts." You must believe in the musicality of your playing to be brave enough to leave space. Andy is so confident in his part that he doesn't play anything on the verses at all! When the chorus arrives, he plays a staccato, ostinato line that pedals a tonic A note below the changing A5–G5–D chords. This gusty move really makes the chorus come to life. If he were to follow the chord progression with roots, it would be just another nice-sounding chorus. By branching out on his own with the pedal tone, he creates a memorable hook all his own.

The most amazing part of Andy's playing in "All Right Now" was saved for the guitar solo. The bass part is so powerful that it actually feels more like a bass solo than a guitar solo. For the tonic chord each time, he plays a line that's derived from his chorus routine. Here, however, he's moved down to the low octave and added a few syncopated sixteenth A notes to spice things up. The use of the open A string is essential because you can't play the following measure without it.

The answer to this phrase appears every other measure in support of the G–D/F♯ progression. Fraser jumps up two octaves and outlines the G chord (root and 5th) and the D chord (major 3rd and root) with low open A notes plucked in between. This tonic A is pervasive throughout the chord sequence, which provides an extremely hip link to the chorus routine. It's almost as if he's combining the bass part (tonic pedal) and the guitar part (chords) of the chorus into one brilliant bass line in support of the guitar solo. Rather than playing the chord tones together, however, he's arpeggiating them, which creates a second melodic hook in addition to the guitar solo. Brilliant stuff for sure!

Vital Stats

Bassist: Andy Fraser

Song: "All Right Now"

Album: *Fire and Water* – Free, 1970

Age at time of recording: 18

Bass: Gibson EB-3

Amp: Marshall amp mixed with a direct feed into the console

Track 12

Chorus
Moderate Rock ♩ = 118

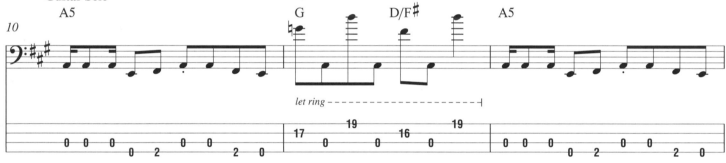

Guitar Solo

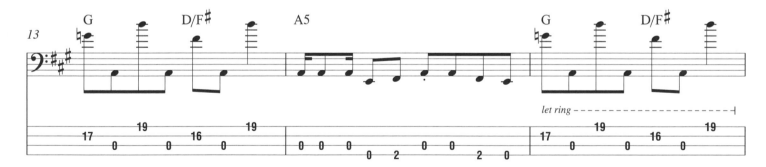

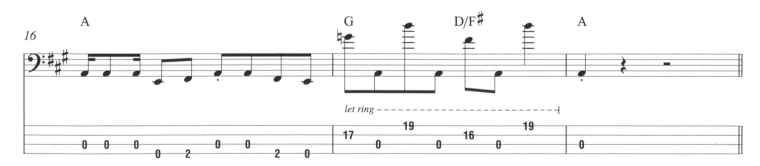

Bootsy Collins

"Sex Machine" is one of the all-time classic funk songs. James Brown recorded it in 1970 as a two-part single on King Records. (The double album of the same name has an eleven-minute version of the song.) "Sex Machine" was one of the first songs James recorded with his then-new band, the J.B.'s. It featured the insistent riffing of Bootsy Collins on bass. With freeform lyrics along with Bobby Byrd's shouts of "Get on up," the song remains harmonically static throughout the whole verse. But the groove is so damned funky, it simply doesn't need anything else. In 2004, *Rolling Stone* magazine ranked "Sex Machine" #326 on the list of the 500 Greatest Songs of All Time.

James Brown lived from 1933 to 2006. Known as the "Godfather of Soul" and the "hardest working man in show business," his legacy is simple: he invented funk, pure and simple. If there were no James Brown, there would be no funk. He was pure dynamite as a performer and a one-of-a-kind creative force in the recording studio. In addition to his music career, James was involved in American political affairs during the volatile sixties and seventies.

James rose from extreme poverty. He shined shoes to pay the bills and along the way taught himself to play the harmonica, guitar, and piano. He ran into trouble with the law at various times in his life, but managed to carve out a brilliant career that spanned several decades. Although he contributed much to the music world through his hit making, James holds a unique place in the record books. He charted the most singles on the Billboard Hot 100 without ever having a #1.

His early recordings were straightforward gospel-inspired R&B compositions influenced by Ray Charles and Little Richard. Billed as James Brown and the Famous Flames, they were not nationally successful until the 1963 album *Live at the Apollo* was released. The album stayed on the pop charts for fourteen months, peaking at #2. James followed with a string of singles that essentially defined the foundation of funk music. Driven by the success of *Live at the Apollo*, he and Famous Flame Bobby Byrd formed a production company to promote sales to white audiences. His 1964 hit "Out of Sight" pointed the way to his later funk hits.

During the mid-sixties, he enjoyed two of his biggest hits, both of which became signature songs: "Papa's Got a Brand New Bag" and "I Got You (I Feel Good)," the former winning a Grammy. Toward the end of the decade, James continued to refine funk with "Cold Sweat," which is often referred to as the first true funk song. Changes that started with "Cold Sweat" also established the musical foundation

> *"James would give you some grunts, and then you'd have to play it back and say, 'Is this what you're talking about?' As long as what you played made him feel good, that was it—whether it was what he meant in the first place or not."*
>
> —Bootsy Collins

Although this album was supposedly recorded live in James's hometown of Augusta, Georgia, there was some debate at the time whether it was indeed "live," since there's a chance that some of the live applause was dubbed.

© Photofest

for later hits like "I Got the Feelin'" and "Mother Popcorn."

By 1970, James and the J.B.'s took the funk to another level with Bootsy Collins on bass. "Sex Machine" was released, and the world of pop music would never be the same. To this day, it can be argued that no funk tune has topped it for pure funkability. Historically speaking, the J.B.'s are considered the greatest of the James Brown bands.

James continued with more funk releases throughout the seventies, including "Get Up Offa That Thang" and "Funky President," but the rise of disco took him off guard. Members of the J.B.'s began to leave, and his star status began to wane. James Brown had one more huge hit in 1985 with the Dan Hartman-penned and produced "Living in America," for which James won a Grammy. He continued to record and perform right up until his death in 2006. His last shows were greeted with positive reviews, and one of his final concert appearances in Ireland drew a crowd of 80,000 people.

William "Bootsy" Collins was born in Cincinnati, Ohio in 1951. Bootsy got his start with James Brown in the late sixties. Bootsy's bass playing propelled James Brown to his glorious heights with funk recordings such as "Super Bad," "Soul Power," "Talkin' Loud and Sayin' Nothing," and the tour de force that is "Sex Machine." Just nineteen years old when he recorded "Sex Machine," he gained prominence as the flamboyant bassist for Parliament-Funkadelic and was inducted as a member of the group in 1997. He pushed the musical envelope even further with Bootsy's Rubber Band. For all the outrageous attire and radical sounds he created with effects, Bootsy is a humble, down-to-earth guy. I met him at the NAMM show, and he was gracious, asked about my friends, and thanked me for being so kind in my praise of his musicianship.

"Get Up (I Feel Like Being a) Sex Machine" was recorded at Starday-King Studios in Nashville, TN. This particular song is notable also because, in comparison to earlier funk hits like "Papa's Got a Brand New Bag" and "Cold Sweat," this song de-emphasizes the horn section. The nucleus rather is Bootsy's bass line, his brother Catfish Collins' guitar groove, and Jabo Starks' drum pocket. Add to this the call and response between James and Bobby Byrd and you have a whole new kind of funk machine.

How to Play It

This bass line can drive you nuts. This is mainly because Bootsy is continually changing a note here and there from the basic routine. Just when you think you have it nailed, he changes it up and messes you up. It takes many listens, but can be had. One of the biggest problems I encounter in others trying to recreate "Sex Machine" is that the bass does not *swing*. The bass must *always* swing in "Sex Machine," so do not miss the swing notation in the top left corner.

The overall phrase outlines a dominant 7th chord (root, low major 3rd, low 5th, and low ♭7th), with the octave root thrown in as well. Pay close attention to the staccato markings, as the groove highly depends on this type of subtlety. Notice how Boosty continues to slightly vary his routine throughout the chorus and verses, maintaining elements of the original line but adding other elements to keep things fresh and alive.

If you can play the verse and chorus, the bridge will play itself. Refer to the notation and play it exactly as written. Don't overplay looking for the right part. It isn't complicated, but if you busy up the bridge it will *sound* complicated and lose its effectiveness. Though the song originally sounds in E♭, I'm convinced it was recorded so the bass could play in the key of D to facilitate the use of open strings during the climbs. It's doubtful that Bootsy was playing in E♭, though it can be done. But, as in "Papa's Got a Brand New Bag," the intuitive nature of the bass line becomes suspect. Try it both ways so you can experience it for yourself and make your own judgment. There is no question that it's easier to play in the D position. My bet is that the bass retuned to play the song, or the tape was sped up after the tracks were recorded. Either scenario is plausible. (For the recording of "Papa's Got a Brand New Bag," the tape was sped up from E♭ to E.)

It's probably a good idea for you to master the song in either key, just to build your chops and make you more versatile. The song is no walk in the park no matter what you try. You have to be strong and quick to be able to play this ferocious groove, but you also must sound relaxed in the pocket. And you can only *sound* relaxed if you *are* relaxed. This comes with lots of slow and steady practice. Find an easy tempo and slowly build up speed over time.

Vital Stats

Bassist: Bootsy Collins

Song: "Get Up (I Feel Like Being a) Sex Machine"

Album: *Sex Machine –* James Brown, 1970

Age at time of recording: 19

Bass: Fender Jazz Bass

Amp: Recorded direct into the mixing console

Track 13

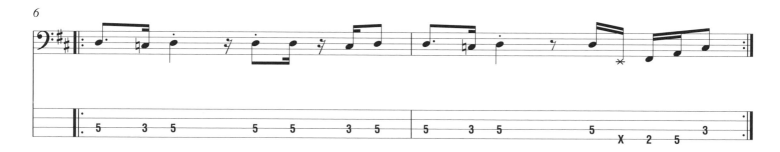

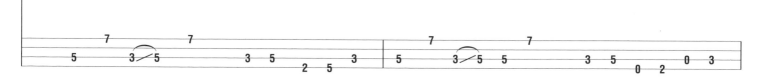

Words and Music by James Brown, Bobby Byrd and Ronald Lenhoff

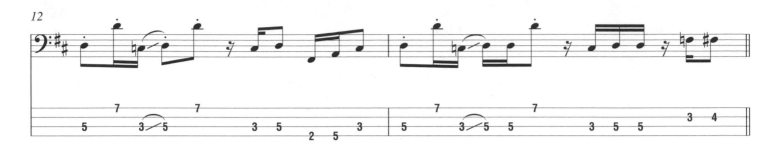

Bridge

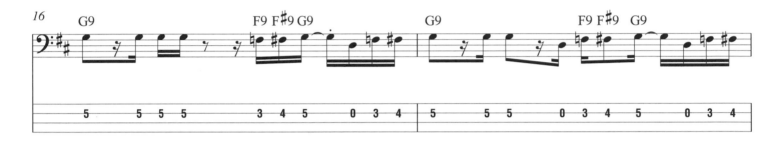

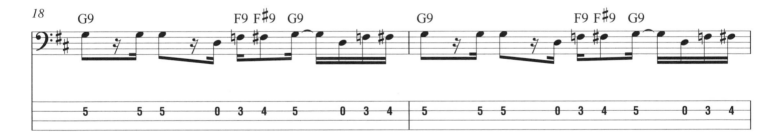

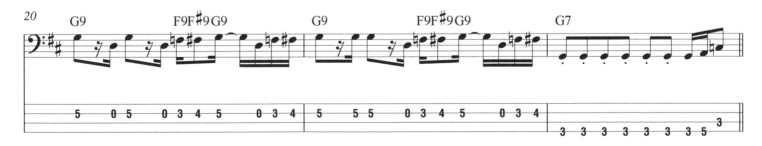

Chorus

James Jamerson

"I used to go out behind the house where there were all these ants on the ground, and I would take a stick and stretch a long rubber band across it and play for the ants. I would make the ants dance."

—James Jamerson

James Jamerson made more than the ants dance when he recorded "What's Going On." He made the whole world dance. Even James himself was impressed with his playing on that song. Word has it, when James returned home from the studio that day, he told his wife Annie, "I just played the greatest bass line of my life."

What's Going On was the first album on which Motown's studio band, the Funk Brothers, received official credit for their work. The album was also the first to reflect the beginning of a new trend of social awareness in soul music. The lyrics spoke about drug use, poverty, and the Vietnam War. *What's Going On* was both an immediate commercial and

critical success and has endured as a classic. It's been voted as one of the landmark recordings in pop music history and is considered to be one of the greatest albums ever made.

The single was actually held up by Motown head, Berry Gordy. Berry was not offended by the politics of the album but was bothered by the album's format, which had each song leading to the next. The flow of sound was unconventional and not suited for radio airplay— Gordy's main focus. The album became known as the first soul music concept album. One of the Motown A&R

© Getty

people secretly got the song to a radio DJ who put it in rotation. The reaction was immediate and overwhelming. Once Gordy saw the commercial potential, he immediately released the song, and the rest is history.

Marvin Gaye was born in 1939 and started out as a session drummer. His vocal range was three octaves, however, and his singing talent was undeniable. Marvin's many other hits included "How Sweet It Is (To Be Loved by You)," "Ain't That Peculiar," "It Takes Two," "Let's Get It On," "Mercy Mercy Me (The Ecology)," "Sexual Healing," "I Heard It Through the Grapevine," and "Ain't No Mountain High Enough." Motown's top selling artist during the sixties, Gaye was ranked #6 in 2008 on *Rolling Stone* magazine's list of the Greatest Singers of All Time.

Motown songwriter Al Cleveland and Four Tops member Renaldo "Obie" Benson wrote "What's Going On," with Marvin adding lyrics and contributing

Gaye was a talented football player, and he was good friends with Mel Farr and Lem Barney, who played for the Detroit Lions. "What's Going On" was an expression they used to greet each other, and Gaye used it as the title. Farr and Barney sang backup on the track.

to the arrangement. Until this song, Marvin Gaye rarely participated in the songwriting process. For this album, he took control of the production so he could make a statement as an artist. Motown was not happy with the idea, but Marvin was an established star and had enough power to pull it off. History has shown it to be a clever move.

How to Play It

"What's Going On" is the culmination of everything Jamerson's bass playing was about: deep groove, melodic drive, and rhythmic virtuosity. In the notation, each measure is thoroughly subdivided so there is no ambiguity whatsoever. No note is to be played for anything in parentheses. Those are merely there to show you where the detailed time is. In fact, when you sound out the rhythm verbally, try to make it a point to *only* sound out the syllables of the notes you play. This method will make you really feel the groove. After lots of practice sounding out rhythmic syllables through a variety of songs, the process of only sounding when notes are to be played

should become intuitive. Take your time with this process. It *will* become automatic to you at some point.

This transcription is very accurate to Jamerson's original bass track. Again, as with the other tricky Jamerson performances, like "Bernadette" and "For Once in My Life," this transcription captures the subtlety and nuance not previously published. Pay particular attention to the use of the open A connecting notes in measures 7, 12, 16, 18, 24, and 38. This is brilliant stuff. When you play the part along with the original recording, your bass will disappear right into the song because these are the subtle details that separate Jamerson's genius from others. At first glance, some of the notes almost seem like wrong notes. They may press the harmonic envelope, but they also economize your left and right hand movements so you can sink deeper into the groove.

The bridge begins in measure 27 with a subtle shift in groove to a light swing and an interesting harmonic turn with Am9. Jamerson subtly acknowledges the 9th in the higher octave in the first measure only, sticking to roots (A), 5ths (E), and octave roots (A) throughout

the remaining Am9 measures. For the extended A/B chord in measures 35–38, he pecks his way through a line mixing notes from a B major arpeggio and the B Mixolydian mode, incorporating plenty of syncopated sixteenths along the way.

Start practicing this tune at an easy tempo until you can play the line with confidence and conviction. There will be a deep sense of accomplishment when you can float through this tune and the groove feels a million miles wide. It will mean one thing: you are a deep groovin' R&B bass player.

Vital Stats

Bassist: James Jamerson

Song: "What's Going On"

Album: *What's Going On* – Marvin Gaye, 1971

Age at time of recording: 35

Bass: 1962 Sunburst Fender Precision Bass ("The Funk Machine")

Amp: Recorded direct into the mixing console

Track 14

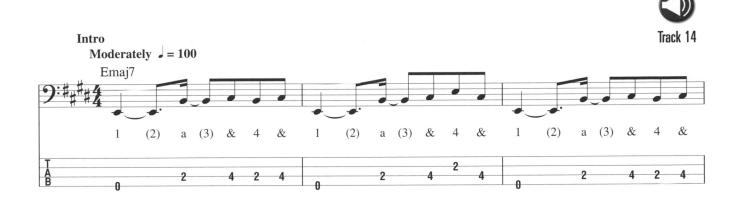

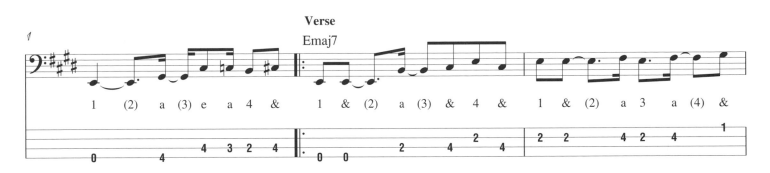

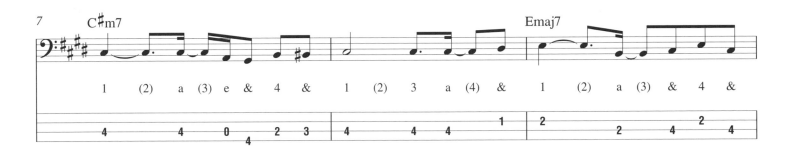

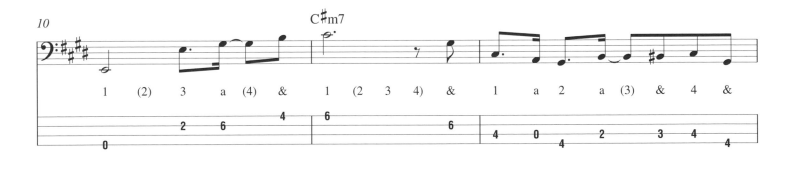

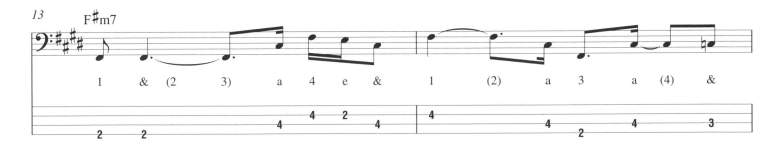

Words and Music by Renaldo Benson, Alfred Cleveland and Marvin Gaye
© 1970 (Renewed 1998) JOBETE MUSIC CO., INC., MGIII MUSIC, NMG MUSIC and FCG MUSIC
All Rights Controlled and Administered by EMI APRIL MUSIC INC. on behalf of JOBETE MUSIC CO., INC., MGIII MUSIC, NMG MUSIC and FCG MUSIC
and EMI BLACKWOOD MUSIC INC. on behalf of STONE AGATE MUSIC (A Division of JOBETE MUSIC CO., INC.)
All Rights Reserved   International Copyright Secured   Used by Permission

What's Going On

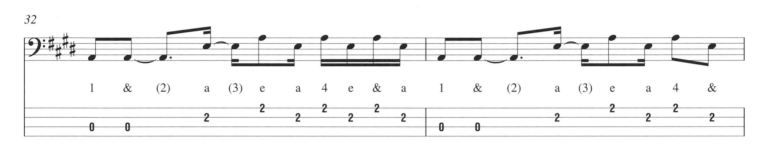

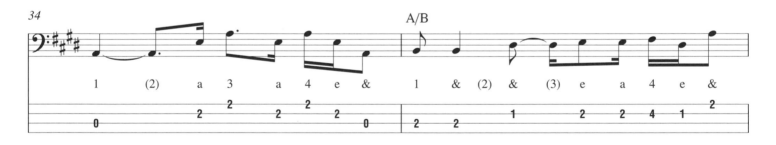

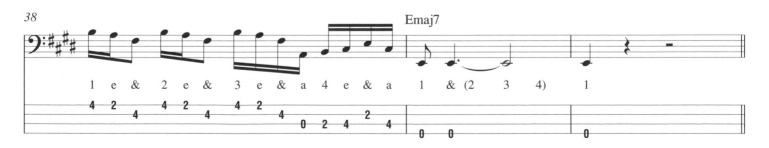

John Entwistle

© Marty Temme

At their peak, the Who was arguably the most powerful live rock 'n' roll band on a concert stage. Their performance and sheer volume were absolutely overwhelming. In 1969, the Who was touring in support of the *Tommy* album (the famed rock opera), and I was lucky enough to score a ticket at the Bushnell Auditorium in Hartford, CT. I have never forgotten that show, for a number of reasons: virtuosic performances (by each band member), amazing showmanship, and earth-shattering volume! We sat in the sixteenth row, and to this day, it was the loudest concert I have ever attended. My ears ached the whole next day.

The Who formed in 1964 in England and were inducted into the Rock and Roll Hall of Fame in 1990—their first year of eligibility. The display there describes them as "Prime contenders, in the minds of many, for the title of World's Greatest Rock Band." They charted 25 Top 20 singles in the UK and/or US and 17 Top 10 albums. They've sold over 100 million records.

The band rose to fame in the UK by pioneering the destruction of their instruments on stage. Their fame grew with memorable performances at the Monterey Pop Festival, Woodstock, and the 1969 release of the rock opera *Tommy*. Keith Moon died in 1978, and in 1983 the band disbanded until the year 2000, when the three surviving members discussed recording an album of new material. The plans were postponed when John Entwistle passed away suddenly in 2002. Townshend and Daltrey continue to perform as the Who and in 2006 released *Endless Wire*. It reached the top ten in both the UK and America.

"Won't Get Fooled Again" was written by Pete Townshend, as were the bulk of the band's songs. In his biography, Pete explained that the song was anti-establishment, but "revolution is not going to change anything in the long run, and people are going to get hurt."

The synthesizer represents the revolution. It builds at the beginning when the uprising starts and comes back at the end when a new revolution is brewing. Roger Daltrey's scream is considered one of the best on any rock song. It was so convincing that the rest of the band, lunching nearby, thought Daltrey was brawling with the engineer. The original version of the song appears as the final track on the *Who's Next* album and spans 8:30. The 1971 single release (a drastically edited version at 3:30 in length) reached #9 in the UK and #15 in the United States Billboard Hot 100.

John Entwistle was born in England in 1944. His early musical training was on trumpet, piano, and French horn, all three of which would figure into his later rock playing. In the early sixties, he played in several jazz and Dixieland bands. He formed the Confederates with his classmate Pete Townshend, after which he joined the Detours with Roger Daltrey, who later became the Who.

His aggressive lead sounding bass playing influenced countless bassists across generations. He typically played pentatonic lines that acted in counterpoint to the melody. His live sound was unusually trebly, partially created by using round wound RotoSound bass strings. It was so bright and upfront, you could easily mistake it for a guitar. The

"With bass, especially bottom end, the vibration has to happen on stage, otherwise the feel is wrong. This is why you can't scale the equipment down too far."

—John Entwistle

This was one of the first times in which a synthesizer was used in the rhythm track. When they played this song live, the Who had to play the synthesizer part off tape.

first time I listened to the *Live at Leeds* album, that's exactly what happened to me. He's famous for playing one of the very first rock bass solos ever recorded: "My Generation" in 1965. To this day, aspiring bassists have been trying to figure that solo out, which can be a daunting task.

He had a most impressive collection of over 200 instruments, including vintage Fender Jazz and Precisions, custom made Alembics, hi-tech Warwicks, as well as various Rickenbackers. He even experimented with and owned all graphite Status basses. The bass used on "Won't Get Fooled Again" was known as "Frankenstein"—a Fender Precision Bass with maple neck with parts from five different Fender basses. It was Entwistle's main stage and studio bass from 1967–1971.

John was nicknamed "The Ox" because he ate, drank, and did more than the rest of the band. Bill Wyman of the Rolling Stones referred to the Ox as "the quietest man in private, but the loudest man on stage." He also earned the nickname "Thunderfingers" because of his blazing

speed. He continually tweaked his stage setup while playing and was one of the first to use Marshall stacks (so he could hear himself over Keith Moon's drumming). He later switched to Sound City and experimented with bi-amping his rig. In bi-amping, the high and low signals are sent through separate amplifiers and speakers, supposedly creating a purer sound. The aesthetic advantage is highly debatable, but it certainly worked for John.

John developed what he called a "typewriter" approach. He positioned his right hand over the strings so *all four* fingers could be used to tap percussively on the strings against the fretboard. This created a distinctively twangy sound. He could play three or four strings at once, or one string with several fingers. He created passages that were both percussive and melodic and could mimic drum fills live, firing them at drummer Keith Moon faster than Moon could play them.

Entwistle is widely considered a pioneer on the bass guitar and has been a tremendous influence on generations of bass players that have followed him. He continues to top "best ever bass player" polls in musician's magazines and, in 2000, he was named "Bassist of the Millennium" by a reader's poll in *Guitar* magazine.

John Entwistle died in a hotel room at the Hard Rock Café in Las Vegas, Nevada in June of 2002, one day before the first show of the Who's 2002 US tour. The medical examiner determined that death was due to a heart attack induced by cocaine. Entwistle was known to have used cocaine much of his adult life.

How to Play It

The initials "AAA" come to mind when describing John Entwistle's playing in this tune: Agility, Aggression, and Aptitude. He plays with a contrapuntal sensibility that weaves around the rest of the music as if he flat out *owns* the song for himself. There has never been another like him and never will be again.

The bass routine starts at the chorus. John cuts right through the A–D/A repeating progression with a melodic use of the A major pentatonic scale, occasionally including a D note from the A major scale. Refer to the notation and tablature for location and rhythmic feel. Roots and 5ths are the order for the G chord beginning in measure 7. For the E chords, he works out of the E minor pentatonic scale to generate a tough, bluesy-sounding line.

He concludes with a descending scalar lick beneath the D chord to the conclusion on A. Don't neglect those slides; they're a big part of the sound. John is bombastic to the end—English hard rock style.

Vital Stats

Bassist: John Entwistle

Song: "Won't Get Fooled Again"

Album: *Who's Next* – The Who, 1971

Age at time of recording: 27

Bass: Entwistle's "Frankenstein" Fender bass

Amp: Recorded direct into the mixing console

Track 15

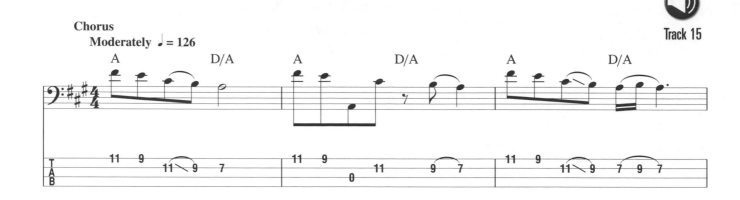

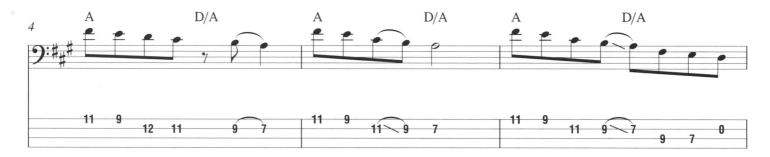

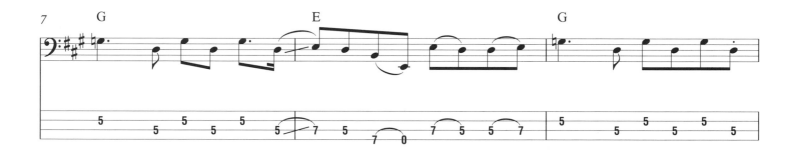

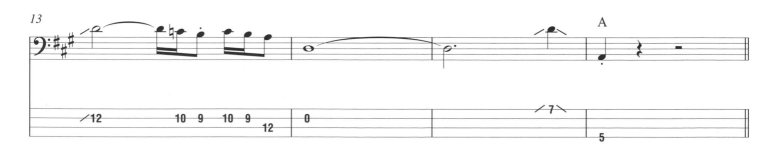

David Hood

"More people ask me about the bass line from 'I'll Take You There' than anything else that I played on."

—David Hood

"I'll Take You There" is a "staple" of music radio. Performed by the Staple Singers and written by their producer, Al Bell, it's from the album *Be Altitude: Respect Yourself* and was released on the Stax record label. It hit #1 and stayed fifteen weeks on the charts. Not a day goes by without this song being in rotation on a radio station somewhere in America. Not a weekend goes by without a cover band somewhere playing this song.

Stax Records president Al Bell (born Alvertis Isbell) wrote this after attending the funeral of his little brother, who was shot to death. "I went out in the backyard in my father's home. And all of a sudden, I heard these lyrics: 'I know a place, ain't nobody worried, ain't nobody crying, and ain't no smiling faces lying to the races, I'll take you there.'"

The Staple Singers were a great gospel, R&B singing group formed by family patriarch Pops Staples. His children Cleotha, Pervis, Yvonne, and Mavis were also members. Their biggest hits were "I'll Take You There," "Respect Yourself," and "Let's Do It Again." "I'll Take You There" features Mavis Staples on lead vocal, as she invites the listeners to seek heaven. The call-and-response chorus and her soulful delivery exude a feel-good vibe that takes the listeners exactly there. In the nineties, the song experienced a revival when Chevy decided to use it in TV commercials. Soon afterward, it was inducted into the Grammy Hall of Fame and is now ranked #276 on the *Rolling Stone* list of 500 Greatest Songs of All Time.

According to engineer Terry Manning and producer/writer Al Bell, the original concept of this song was to combine elements of Jamaican reggae with R&B. In fact, the intro is lifted from a Jamaican instrumental titled "The Liquidator." Whatever their intentions, the mission was accomplished; this tune will outlive us all. Legendary session bassist David Hood, of the famed Muscle Shoals, recorded live with only a direct box and his trusty Fender bass.

The Muscle Shoals Sound Studio in Muscle Shoals, Alabama was formed in 1969 when musicians Barry Beckett (keyboards), Roger Hawkins (drums), Jimmy Johnson (guitar), and David

© Getty

Hood left FAME Studios to create their own. They were the first rhythm section to own their own studio, publishing, and production companies. The Muscle Shoals sound was nothing short of brilliant, and their special arrangement and accompaniment style was sought out by Wilson Pickett, Aretha Franklin, and many more, resulting in innumerable legendary recordings.

David Hood is at the top of the list in recording session accomplishments and has played on countless tracks over the years. Artists include Traffic, Rod Stewart, Wilson Pickett, Aretha Franklin, Boz Scaggs, Linda Ronstadt, Laura Nyro, Albert King, Jimmy Cliff, Paul Simon, Bobby Womack, Willie

Nelson, Bob Seger, Simon & Garfunkel, Johnnie Taylor, Kim Carnes, Cat Stevens, Dr. Hook, Delbert McClinton, Eddie Rabbitt, James Brown, the Oak Ridge Boys, Julian Lennon, Carlos Santana, Glenn Frey, Sawyer Brown, Bobby "Blue" Bland, Etta James, and Connie Francis.

His bass solo in "I'll Take You There" is a lesson in what to play and how to play it. I spoke with him about this masterful track and told him I wanted to include his solo in *25 Great Bass Lines*, he said he was "honored and humbled."

"More people ask me about the bass line from 'I'll Take You There' than anything else that I played on. The song, which was brought to us by Stax Records producer Al Bell, was first played to us as an instrumental demo track. We were told to try to improve on the drums and bass line, but keep the basic 'Island' feel. Years later, we were surprised to find out that the demo that we heard was actually a commercially released record by Jamaican group Harry J's Allstars, called 'The Liquidator.'

"The solo was inspired by the intro and solo on the Staple's 'Respect Yourself.' Our keyboard player, Barry Beckett (Mavis calls out to him in the song), suggested the melody idea for the solo, and I just played my version of that. Incidentally, when Mavis calls out 'Daddy' in reference to Pops, she originally said Eddie in reference to Eddie Hinton who was playing the electric guitar solo. I was about 28 years old at the time and had been playing for ten years. I was playing my first and only bass, which was a 1961 stacked-pot Fender Jazz Bass.

"I played through a late sixties Fender Bassman piggy-back amp, which was miked with an RCA 44. They also took

a direct signal to the board, and that is probably what is heard on that record as they would usually run out of tracks and lose the miked bass track."

How to Play It

Hand motion economics and chord theory knowledge are essential for this tune. Use minimal fretting hand movements to execute this bass part. David Hood's bass line *sounds* much easier than it is. Use proper right- and left-hand technique, practice daily, and you will be "taking us there" before you know it.

The solo section is played *legato* (smooth and connected, with no perceptible spaces of silence between all notes). C major and F major triads alternate every measure. A major chord consists of the root, major 3rd, and perfect 5th of a given major scale. So a C major chord contains C (root), E (major 3rd), and G (perfect 5th). An F major chord contains F (root), A (major 3rd), and C (perfect 5th). This is the key to building this bass solo.

The solo starts on the 3rd of C (E). This makes the solo feel *melodic* right away because the first note of the solo is not the root of the chord. Melodic phrases often begin on harmonic intervals (3rd, 5th, 7th, etc.). If your solo starts on the root, it won't grab the listener as much. Try it and you will find out for yourself.

Be sure to pay attention to the grace notes in this solo, because they really help lend a melodic tone to the bass—especially up in the higher register. There are two different ones: from G (5th) to A (6th) in the C measure, and from E (7th) to F (root) in the F measures. Most importantly, *rake* through those

descending notes with one finger of your plucking hand. The rake down through the F chord in measure 2 will actually begin on the high G (last note played on the C chord in the previous measure). So you'll play four notes (one on each string) with one finger on your plucking hand. Talk about bass economics 101!

Now move back to a C chord for the second half of the solo routine. After the octave–5th–root rake, shift to F's major 3rd (A at fret 12 of the A string) with the 3rd finger of your fretting hand to set up the next phrase. Play the solo routine again, but be sure to take the second ending. Notice that the low C at the beginning of measure 6 functions as the 5th of the F chord again, which is a beautiful harmony note.

This solo is a classic example of economy of note choices with maximum aesthetic impact. Words of wisdom: start and end a solo *not* on a root, but on a chord tone. If you use this method, you have a pretty good chance of creating a phrase that is melodic, harmonic, and most importantly, easy to follow.

Vital Stats

Bassist: David Hood

Song: "I'll Take You There"

Album: *Be Altitude: Respect Yourself* – The Staple Singers, 1972

Age at time of recording: 28

Bass: 1961 Fender Jazz Bass

Amp: '60s Fender Bassman used to monitor, but recorded direct in the mixing console

Bass Solo
Moderately ♩ = 101

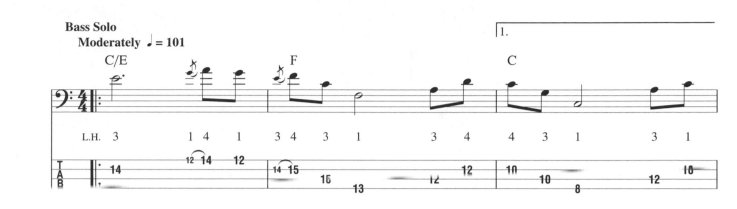

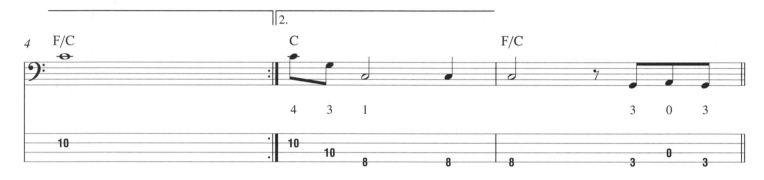

Chorus

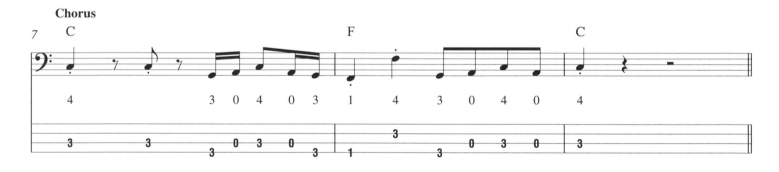

Randy Jo Hobbs

The Edgar Winter Group was arguably one of the best American pop-rock groups of the early seventies. Led by virtuoso jazz and blues musician Edgar Winter, they were one of the hottest arena rock bands to tour the world. Their intense concerts featured virtuoso performances from Edgar on keyboards, saxophones, and vocals.

They released the legendary album, *They Only Come out at Night* in 1973, produced by Rick Derringer. It peaked at #3 on the Billboard Hot 200 and stayed on the charts for an impressive 80 weeks. It featured the Grammy-winning #1 hit "Frankenstein," which pioneered the use of the synthesizer as a lead instrument. The follow-up single, written by group bassist Dan Hartman, was "Free Ride." It reached #14 on the singles charts and contains all the elements of a great pop song: infectious melody, great

Edgar Winter

> *"He was a great, great player. He was one of the best bass players you could ever think of. Everybody recognized that in Randy Hobbs."*
>
> —guitarist Rick Derringer

harmonies, a high-energy drum groove, a great guitar hook, and a very funky bass line played by Randy Jo Hobbs.

"Free Ride" still pops up just about anywhere and everywhere: classic rock radio, TV commercials, retail store muzak, and DJ nightclubs. Music critics have noted a Sly & the Family Stone influence on the writing of "Free Ride," as the melody is strong on gospel and funk. The tune feels like a rock and roll revival meeting.

Edgar is a brilliant perfectionist, but Dan's talent and hit sensibility propelled them to commercial success. Actually, he wrote "Free Ride" before he was a member of the Edgar Winter Group. He sent it to Steve Paul, Edgar's manager, in a demo package and was asked to join

the band. Though he's most famous as the bassist and singer of the Edgar Winter Group, he later enjoyed solo success with the disco hit "Instant Replay" and the eighties hit "I Can Dream About You." Dan also wrote and produced the James Brown (see "Get Up [I Feel Like Being a] Sex Machine") classic, "Living in America." Sadly, Dan passed away in 1994 at the age of 43 from an AIDS-related illness.

During the early days of the Edgar Winter Group, Dan was not the bassist. In fact, he shared guitar chores with Ronnie Montrose. Randy Jo Hobbs was the bassist on the "Free Ride" recording session but left the group before the first album was completed. Dan then took over on bass. As a teenager, Randy was the

"Free Ride" and "Frankenstein" were smash hits from the album, They Only Come Out at Night. *Actually "Frankenstein" got its name because it was pieced together from many recorded tape splicings. Drummer Chuck Ruff commented "Woh! It's like a Frankenstein."*

bassist in the McCoys during the sixties. They were most famous for the #1 hit "Hang on Sloopy," which was sung by sixteen-year-old Rick Derringer. Randy's playing credits include Edgar Winter's *White Trash Roadwork* album and several albums for blues guitarist Johnny Winter (Edgar's older brother and first "find" of manager Steve Paul). He also played on *Jump on It* by Montrose in 1976.

The Edgar Winter Group was a musician's band, and Randy Jo Hobbs was a musician's bass player. The music-buying public loved this band, and musicians respected them as much as they were loved. I wore out my Johnny and Edgar Winter vinyl albums trying to figure out what Randy Jo Hobbs was playing. His lines were equal parts rock, blues, funk, and spontaneity. Simply put, he is one the best, and his accomplishments must be studied. You'll be a better musician for doing so. Randy tragically died in 1993 of a drug-related heart failure in a hotel room in Dayton,

Ohio. He's buried in his hometown of Union City, Indiana.

Though "Free Ride" had been demoed previously, Randy Jo Hobbs, with his nimble funkiness, made the bass line all his own. Edgar Winter, who had no problem tracing Randy's groove, doubled the bass on clavinet.

How to Play It

"Free Ride" can be played fingerstyle or pick-style, but Randy played it with a pick. If you have your picking technique down, you can easily play this part with a little practice. Refer to the notation and tablature for exact notes and fretboard location.

Special Tip

Here's a quick primer in picking technique. For steady eighth notes, downbeats get downstrokes, and upbeats get upstrokes. For sixteenth notes, this motion is doubled. If you keep "double time" with your plucking wrist, you can master the technique. Refer to my book *Stuff! Good Bass Players Should Know* (Hal Leonard) for more details about picking technique.

It's not so much the notes as it is the *rhythm of the notes* that makes the song percolate. Stripped down, the bass plays the roots of chords, along with descending and ascending scalar passing tones. But the funk is hidden inside the sixteenth notes. Keep a close watch on the notation and tablature. Everything is right there. The syncopated sixteenth

notes make this bass line very funky. I've subdivided the verse with added counting so there is no doubt where the funk lays. You must understand that "1 e and a" breaks a beat down into four equal parts. Everything lies within the first five frets of your bass, so don't go hunting all over the neck. This will keep movements very economical and make it easier to get inside the pocket.

Some players omit the chromatic walk down from A to F♯ right before the chorus. Additionally, players forget to play the sixteenth pick up notes E and F♯ into the G chord and/or F♯ and G into the A chord at the start of the chorus. Don't neglect these details if you want to sound authentic playing this song. Also, don't forget the double-stop power chord (root and 5th) that concludes the chorus. You'll have a lot of fun learning and playing this song. Take your time and start out slowly before you try to play at album tempo.

Vital Stats

Bassist: Randy Jo Hobbs

Song: "Free Ride"

Album: *They Only Come out at Night* – The Edgar Winter Group, 1972

Age at time of recording: 24

Bass: '60s Fender Jazz Bass

Amp: Recorded direct into the mixing console

Track 17

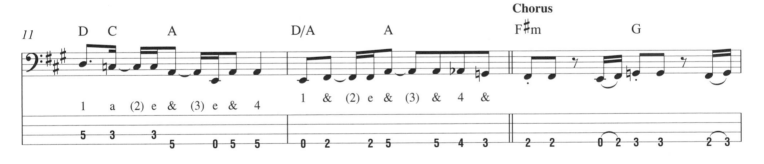

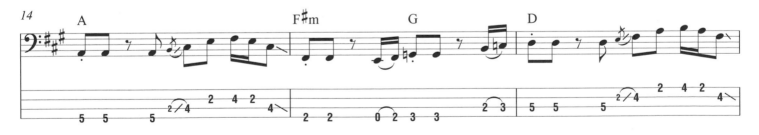

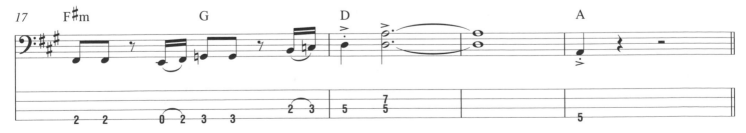

Words and Music by Dan Hartman

Herbie Flowers

© Getty

"Walk on the Wild Side" was written by Lou Reed, chief songwriter of the pioneering sixties band, Velvet Underground. The song appeared on his 1972 solo album *Transformer*, which was produced by David Bowie. Widely received, despite the controversial subject matter dealing with transsexuals, prostitutes, and oral sex, it reached #16 on Billboard Hot 100 in the States and #10 in the UK. It ranks 221 on *Rolling Stone* magazine's list of the 500 Greatest Songs of All Time.

"Walk on the Wild Side" is particularly noted for its two bass lines—one on upright bass and one on fretless electric—both played by Herbie Flowers. This musical concept had never been tried by anyone in popular music before Herbie. Typical of Lou Reed compositions, the chord progression consists of only the I and IV chords (C and F).

After John Paul Jones (before his Led Zeppelin career), Herbie Flowers is the best-known session bassist in England. He's also among a small group of rock musicians whose musical career included military service. Drafted into the Royal Air Force, Herbie decided against combat training and chose to serve in the RAF Central Band. He studied tuba (the military version of the bass) and was a member of the RAF band for nine years.

After he was discharged from the service, he played in several Dixieland bands. He gravitated toward modern jazz, took up the standup bass, and quit Dixieland jazz. In the early sixties, Herbie got a gig playing in a band on the Queen Elizabeth ocean liner. This took him to New York City, where he heard jazz being played on the electric bass guitar. He then quit the upright and bought himself a Fender Jazz bass at the legendary Manny's Musicland on West 48th Street off Times Square in Manhattan.

Back in England, he quickly became one of the most in-demand players of his day. His bass playing can be heard

"How remarkable is Lou Reed's 'Walk on the Wild Side' without that string bass part provided by Herbie Flowers?"

—David Hepworth, rock journalist and writer

on albums by Elton John, David Bowie, David Essex, Al Kooper, Cat Stevens, Harry Nilsson, and many others. It has been said that Herbie Flowers played on over 500 hit records.

Herbie recorded two solo albums: *Plant Life* (1975, Philips Records) and *A Little Potty*. Neither were very successful. In the latter part of the seventies, he formed the band Sky with some of the top players of the day. In spite of the workload with Sky, he continued his session work and also began working on movie soundtracks, as well as orchestral pieces.

With all his studio credits, Herbie Flowers is most noted for his hip, never-heard-before double-tracked basses on "Walk on the Wild Side." He was paid 17 pounds for the session back in 1972. The fact that he added a second instrument (bass guitar) allowed him to be paid for two sessions. (Had he double tracked his part on just the upright bass that would not have happened.)

Herbie's unforgettable bass part for "Walk on the Wild Side" gave rise to the "Herbie Flowers Argument." Stated so aptly by David Hepworth: "How remarkable is Lou Reed's 'Walk on the Wild Side' without that string bass part provided by Herbie?" Should musicians who make significant contributions but don't write the song still benefit from the revenue as the songwriter does? Many such contributions are financially unrecognized. The rare exception occurs if the songwriter is particularly magnanimous. It seems as though 17 pounds is hardly commensurate with Herbie's contribution to "Walk on the

Wild Side." It's difficult to imagine that song being successful without the upright and fretless bass parts.

How to Play It

One's ear is instantly drawn to the infectious intertwining of two distinct bass lines occurring simultaneously. Bassists from all walks of life give kudos to Herbie Flowers for "Walk on the Wild Side." The upright bass pattern throughout the song is plenty to carry the song. The fretless overdub, however, elevates the song from novel interest to "a song for all time." "Walk on the Wild Side" goes straight to the bass hall of fame. Herbie knew where that fretless line would take the song, so he took his fretless bass out of its case and created musical magic.

You cannot create a bass part like this without an understanding of harmony theory. The chord progression on the chorus is basic enough—C to F—and the upright handles the roots of each chord. The fretless plays the major 3rd of the C chord (high E) and slides up to the major 3rd of the F chord (high A). It then moves to the perfect 5th of F (high C) before sliding back down to the major 3rd of the C chord to begin the cycle again. What makes this part even more dynamic is the contrary motion. Notice that when the upright moves down from C to low F, the fretless slides up from high E to high A. Conversely, when the upright returns from low F up to C, the fretless slides down from high C to high E.

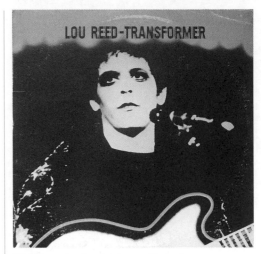

This song is about transvestites who come to New York City and become prostitutes. "Take a walk on the wild side" is what they say to potential customers. Each verse introduces a new character—Holly, Candy, Little Joe, Sugar Plum Fairy, and Jackie—all cronies of the infamous Andy Warhol Factory, as was Lou.

For fun, you can try executing both parts at the same time with a two-hand tapping method. Your fretting hand would tap the low C and low F chord roots, and your plucking hand would have to tap the sliding high chord tones. Try using your middle finger to execute those slides. You might get more power and articulate notes, but experiment and see what works best for you. It can be done with a little effort, so give it a try!

Vital Stats

Bassist: Herbie Flowers

Song: "Walk on the Wild Side"

Album: *Transformer* – Lou Reed, 1972

Age at time of recording: 34

Bass: '60s Fender Jazz fretless bass and upright bass

Amp: Fender bass recorded direct into the mixing console, upright bass was miked

Track 18

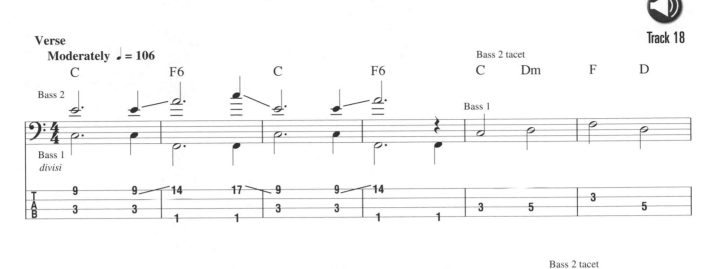

Roger Waters

"Either you write songs or you don't. And if you do write songs like I do, I think there's a natural desire to want to make records."
—Roger Waters

© Photofest

Roger Waters was born in 1943 in Surrey, England. He was the chief creative force in Pink Floyd from 1965 to 1983. In the beginning, they initially earned recognition for their psychedelic music, which later evolved into more of a progressive rock. Pink Floyd is known for thoughtful lyrics, sonic exploration, creative album cover artwork, and elaborately staged concert performances. The group has sold over 200 million albums worldwide, including 75 million in the United States, and has influenced a generation of progressive rock groups, such as Yes, Genesis, Nine Inch Nails, and Dream Theater.

Pink Floyd formed in London in 1965. The group enjoyed moderate success in the early days, but when guitarist David Gilmour joined the band and Roger Waters became a dominant writer,

things really took off commercially. The band's crowning achievement is thought by many to be *Dark Side of the Moon*, released in 1973. With Roger writing all the lyrics and part of the music, it became one of the most successful albums in rock history. Waters is the sole author of the album's Top 10 hit, "Money." His role as

main songwriter continued on subsequent Pink Floyd records, such as *Wish You Were Here* (1975), *Animals* (1977), and *The Wall* (1979). He wrote all of *The Final Cut* (1983). All sold millions.

In 1985, Waters quit the band, but Pink Floyd continued with the other members. Roger sued them for the name, and

This song is about the bad things money can bring. Ironically, it made Pink Floyd lots of cash, as the album sold over 34 million copies. This is often misinterpreted as a tribute to money. Many people thought the line "Money, it's a gas," meant Floyd considered money a very good thing.

both sides reached a settlement out of court allowing David Gilmour and the others to continue as Pink Floyd. Without Waters, the band had continued success as Roger pursued a solo career of moderate success, releasing several albums along the way. Twenty years later though, Roger Waters performed live with Pink Floyd in July of 2005 at the London Live 8 concert.

The demo for "Money," including sound effects, was recorded in a basic studio in Roger's garden shed. The demo was unlike the bluesy, transatlantic feel of the full band recording on *Dark Side of the Moon*. Though credited solely to Waters, the instrumental jam was in fact a group effort, and David Gilmour's input on the arrangement is obvious on the final product. The song was a cornerstone of Pink Floyd's live performances, and Roger continued to perform the song on his solo tours.

One of the few worldwide hits to make use of an odd time signature, a seven-beat loop of monetary related sound effects opens the song. "Money" is based on the standard 12-bar blues—a Bm blues in this case. The song begins in an unusual 7/4 time signature, changes to 4/4 during the guitar solo, and then returns to 7/4 before ending in 4/4 on another jam.

When *Guitar World* asked Dave Gilmour in February of 1993 where the famous time signature for "Money" came from, he replied: "It's Roger's riff. Roger came in with the verses and lyrics for more or less completed. And we just made up middle sections, guitar solos, and all that stuff. We also invented some new riffs—we created a 4/4 progression for the guitar solo and made the poor saxophone player play in 7/4. It was my idea to break down and become dry and empty for the second chorus of the solo." Interestingly, Roger Waters is the only songwriter credited, but the lead vocal is by David Gilmour.

How to Play It

Hint: How to Count Odd Time Signatures

This song is not difficult to play, but it might be difficult to *feel* the counting. You can do this one of two ways. You can count mathematically: 1 2 3 4 5 6 7, 1 2 3 4 5 6 7, etc. Or, you can count to seven by listening to the *shape* of the bass phrase and count musically. In this song, the seven-beat riff has two mini riffs inside it. The first is a three count (B, B–F♯, B), and the second is a four count (F♯–A–B–D). This totals seven beats, and that gets you through the measure of 7/4. So, you can alternatively count the first

four measures like this: 1 2 3 1 2 3 4, 1 2 3 1 2 3 4, etc. Whenever you encounter a riff with an odd time signature, listen inside the measure for smaller riffs. In most cases, your ear will find these riffs and allow you to find a more *intuitive* way to count so you do not get lost.

Be sure to notice the fret-hand finger choices. Faithfully following the tablature will allow you to play this song with maximum economy. When playing any root, octave, 5th pattern, *always* play the root with your index finger, the octave with your pinky, and the 5th with your ring finger. Make this routine into an exercise that you play everyday over and over again. (The only exception is when an open string is involved, as in measure 7.) The best technique is when neither the listener nor the player notices it. They just hear *music*. That is always the goal.

In measure 5, the meter changes to 4/4 time for three measures and 2/4 for one measure, so pay attention and continue to use the root/5th/octave fingering. Also, be sure you *rake* those descending notes with your plucking finger. Failure to do so is fatal to your groove.

Vital Stats

Bassist: Roger Waters

Song: "Money"

Album: *Dark Side of the Moon* – Pink Floyd, 1973

Age at time of recording: 30

Bass: Fender Precision bass

Amp: Recorded direct into the mixing console

Track 19

Verse

Moderately slow ♩ = 71

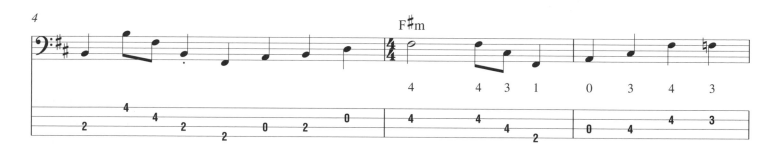

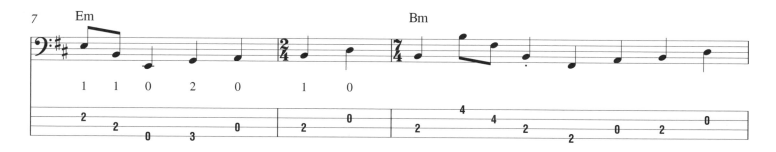

Tom Hamilton

Aerosmith is one of the great American rock bands. The band is still going strong in the twenty-first century with all the original members—singer Steven Tyler, guitarists Joe Perry and Brad Whitford, drummer Joey Kramer, and bassist Tom Hamilton. They are the best-selling American rock band of all time, with over 150 million albums sold. The band has scored twenty-one Top 40 hits, four Grammy Awards, and ten MTV Video Music Awards. They were inducted into the Rock and Roll Hall of Fame in 2001, and in 2005 they were ranked #57 in *Rolling Stone* magazine's 100 Greatest Artists of All Time.

By the end of the seventies, they had emerged as one of the most popular hard rock bands in the world. However, drug addiction and internal conflict took

"Aerosmith may be the kind of rock band that requires meat-and-potatoes bass support, but Tom Hamilton proves just how tasty that menu can be."

—Bill Leigh, editor of *Bass Player* magazine

© Marty Temme

their toll. Joe Perry and Brad Whitford quit in 1979 and 1981, respectively. Replacing them with Jimmy Crespo and Rick Dufay, the band released *Rock in a Hard Place*. It went gold but failed to match their previous success. Perry and Whitford returned in 1984, and the band signed a new deal with Geffen Records. When the band finally sobered up in 1987 and released *Permanent Vacation*, they regained their previous stature. Throughout the late eighties and nineties, Aerosmith enjoyed a stream of hits and awards for music from *Pump* (1989), *Get a Grip* (1993), and *Nine Lives* (1997). Their comeback is one of the most remarkable in rock history. After forty years of performing, they are a train that still keeps a rollin'.

Tom Hamilton was born in Colorado Springs, Colorado in 1951. He began playing guitar at age twelve but switched to bass because the one and only local band needed a bassist. Steven Tyler discovered Tom along with guitarist

Joe Perry playing in the Jam Band at Lake Sunapee, New Hampshire. Tom's bass playing style is typically that of a supporting role. Aerosmith's music features foremost the screaming blues-inflected vocals of Steven Tyler and the scorching riff-based guitar work of Joe Perry, but that's not to say Tom Hamilton's bass lines are not inventive and integral to the Aerosmith sound. Quite the contrary, his playing makes their wall of sound style very *listenable*. Such a style is an art unto itself.

According to *Rolling Stone's* Top 500 Singles, "As the sessions for *Toys in the Attic* reached the eleventh hour at the Record Plant in New York, producer Douglas called out for ideas. Bassist Hamilton resurrected a riff that had been germinating for several years, and it was outfitted with bass marimba and Joe Perry's voice-box recitation of the song title. A few months later, Aerosmith had their first Top 40 single."

How to Play It

Ironically, "Sweet Emotion," written by Tom Hamilton and Steven Tyler, is not just a simple hard rock bass part tethered to the kick drum. It is a clever and deft bit of bass playing that's eluded many aspiring bassists. Few if any have ever nailed the routine note for note. Part of the reason for that is the bass part was composed with a pick. Tom Hamilton is fluent with both fingers and a pick. The bass line to "Sweet Emotion" plays out very intuitively if you play pick style correctly. However, it can (and should) be learned using both techniques. This will diversify your playing and make you more comfortable no matter the situation.

Hint: How to Play Pick-Style

Pick-style bass playing is identical to guitar picking. The basic rule of thumb (or pick) is this: downbeats get downstrokes, and upbeats get upstrokes. If you're playing sixteenth notes, just double-time the concept. If you play a routine that has some eighth notes

In the movie Be Cool *starring John Travolta, Steven Tyler is asked what he was thinking when he wrote "Sweet Emotion." Tyler agreed that it was the pure, sweet emotion that he experienced with his young daughters.*

and some sixteenth notes, your plucking hand moves as if you are playing all sixteenth notes. In other words, keep your plucking hand moving to keep time. You'll be purposefully "missing" on some strokes so that you're still pairing the "ones" and the "ands" with downstrokes and the "e's" and the "a's" with upstrokes. It's not that difficult, but it does take slow, disciplined practice to master the routine. You won't be able to play pick-style in a day, but you might in a few weeks if you practice daily.

Hint: Fingerstyle Technique

Refer to the notation and tablature. When learning fingerstyle, start with your second finger. Many bass players learning fingerstyle have discovered if they start with their second finger, they will alternate more easily. You must be disciplined and faithful to these plucking-hand finger choices if you want to be successful playing this demanding bass line. Visually inspect your plucking hand while playing this part so you do not vary your fingerings. If you only watch your fretting hand, you probably won't be plucking with the correct fingers. Work hard and practice this routine *every day*. Be disciplined with your plucking fingerings, and you *will* be successful.

It helps to know chords when playing "Sweet Emotion" because the bass line is based off an arpeggio of A7 and an A7sus4. The chord tones of an A7 chord are: root (A), major 3rd (C#), 5th (E), and ♭7th (G). An A7sus4 chord is a *suspended* chord. That means you *suspend* the major 3rd (C#) and substitute it with the 4th (D). The suspended chord creates *tension*, and that tension is followed by *release*. In this case, that means to follow with the *unsuspended* chord, or A7. The

"Amen" refrain sung in church is the most obvious use of this 4-3 suspension.

The bass part to "Sweet Emotion" almost sounds like it is a guitar part. This is because Tom Hamilton plays it up an octave at the twelfth fret on the A string. Additionally, he is playing with a pick, and his bass EQ is set to accentuate the treble frequencies. Once you discover the bass is playing that wickedly fast groove, the realization sets in that it's going to take a lot of work. Be prepared to practice long and hard if you want to master this song.

The verse, when dissected, is almost just as cool. It's a less obtrusive bass part, but it's much more interesting than pedaling a low open A. The bass line is in total counterpoint to the guitar line. Masterfully, it slurs up to the tonic chord (A) from the low ♭7th and dances to the octave and back. Interestingly, the open A is hit on the "and" of beat 1 in each measure. This subliminally differentiates the timbre of the low open A from the fretted low A.

The verse concludes with a classic Aerosmith riff, played in unison by the guitars and bass. This type of bluesy riff has been done a million times, but never like this before. Check out the use of the low open E and the chromatic climb back up to the tonic A. It doesn't get any cooler than this.

Vital Stats

Bassist: Tom Hamilton

Song: "Sweet Emotion"

Album: *Toys in the Attic* – Aerosmith, 1975

Age at time of recording: 24

Bass: Fender Jazz Bass

Amp: Recorded direct into the mixing console

Track 20

Bernard Edwards

© Getty

"Bernard was one of those very magical people that the sound that you hear is actually in his fingers, and it doesn't make any difference what bass he plays."

—guitarist Nile Rodgers

Bernard Edwards was born in 1952 in Greenville, North Carolina, and is one of the all-time greatest bass players, hands down. As the saying goes, "It's never the bass, but always the bass player," and Bernard's soul emanated through whatever brand or model bass he played. His career began with his partnership to guitarist Nile Rodgers, with whom he formed the Big Apple Band based in New York. Later, in the mid seventies, with the addition of Tony Thompson on drums, Chic was born.

Chic is widely considered the finest of the disco-era bands. They enjoyed commercial success with hit after hit. But Chic was equally respected and admired by musicians everywhere. "Good Times" unintentionally kick-started the hip-hop phenomenon when the Sugarhill Gang released "Rapper's Delight." It was a direct rip of "Good Times." The validity of rap can be debated, but the bass line to "Rapper's Delight" cannot. The case is closed on Bernard Edwards. He was a badass.

The massive success Chic experienced brought lucrative production offers to Bernard and his songwriting partner, Chic guitarist Nile Rodgers. "We Are Family," made famous by Sister Sledge, was produced and written by Bernard and Nile. Kim Sledge comments, "When we saw the kinds of things they were doing, it worked. They are geniuses."

As a bassist, Bernard Edwards was *automatic*. Legend has it that Bernard never had to punch in (repair) his bass part, even on extended-length dance tracks. Clearly, he was a pro's pro. Years ago, I watched the documentary on the supergroup Power Station recording their album (produced by Bernard Edwards) on MTV. John Taylor, the bass player, was trying to get the hang of the slap bass line for "Bang a Gong" (a remake of the T. Rex classic). Bernard asked for the bass and told the engineer to roll tape. He then laid down a slap groove that was pure pocket. Being so familiar with his style, I am convinced Bernard's part is on the finished product. Sadly, Bernard passed away from pneumonia while on tour in Japan with a reunited Chic in 1996.

One of the most popular disco songs of all time, it is a joyful look back at the roller-disco decade when, after Nixon, Vietnam, and recession, better days seemed to be ahead.

How to Play It

They key to playing "Good Times" on bass is familiarity with the diatonic modes. Specifically, the Dorian mode is the basis for this bass line. Dorian is a type of minor scale. Think of it as a minor scale with a natural 6th instead of a ♭6th. Or, you can just start a major scale on the 2nd and play to an octave above that. Though the key signature for "Good Times" shows E minor, the song is actually in a modal key of E Dorian. If you play the notes of a D major scale starting and ending on E, you'll have E Dorian. Don't forget to include F♯ and C♯.

Intervals

You should be thinking *intervals* when you play this mode (number names for notes). There are two definitions for every mode. You must think what interval of the major scale the mode starts on. The Dorian mode starts on the major 2nd interval of a major scale—D major scale in this case. This is the macrocosmic definition, because you relate the scale back to the key from which it is derived. In other words, E Dorian is the D major scale starting and ending on the 2nd interval.

Here's the microcosmic definition: Look at this E Dorian mode as a kind of E scale. Take the E minor scale and raise the 6th from C to C♯. You now have a half step (one fret) between the 2nd and the ♭3rd and a half step between the major 6th and the ♭7th. This is a bluesy-sounding minor scale that shows up in rock, jazz, and pop all the time. Try to remember what the intervals sound like *and* what they

look like. So, when you are in E Dorian, you *visualize* the intervals as well as hear them. You know where the notes are on the fingerboard, and you know what the notes sound like.

Chic Technique

Think E Dorian and you are ready to play the hook (chorus) bass line to "Good Times." It's very percussive, so make those three low E notes short and crisp (note the staccato dots in notation). Next, hop up the scale to middle E, and rake down to the open A with the same plucking finger as the band moves to the A7 chord. It is absolutely essential you rake this with the same finger. Do NOT pluck the open A with a different finger; you will lose the feel, and the groove will die.

At this point, the harmony moves from Em7 to A7. This is where you pedal the root to, and then between, the major 6th and minor 7th. It's a classic honky-tonk left-hand piano line and works beautifully here. The raking is quick so take your time to sort through it before you bring it up to speed. Don't forget to be as economical as possible with your plucking fingers. Be sure to use the same finger when going from the D string back to the A string. Also, on the A7 chord, be sure to keep your fingers on your fretting hand close together. If you don't, harmonics will start chiming seemingly out of nowhere. The riff concludes with a return to E.

If you think of Em7 to A7 as a ii–V chord progression in the key of D, you are correct. That's technically true. But the tonic of "Good Times" is E. Thus, you could also think of this progression as a i (Em)–IV (A7). Both are technically

correct, but be sure to remember that E is the tonal center.

Enunciate and Articulate

The "Good Times" verse groove is a slightly more simplified bass line, but it's nonetheless very effective. It pulses chord roots, deftly bouncing off the ♭7th to the octave. The move to the A7 chord climbs via the ♭3rd to the root (A). Crisp and precise technique makes this bass line continue to control the song's rhythmic direction. Be sure to continue gaining more *control* over your bass. Take your time so the notes *enunciate* and *articulate*. Gradually build up your tempo day by day so the control remains intact as you increase speed.

Vital Stats

Bassist: Bernard Edwards

Song: "Good Times"

Album: *Risqué* – Chic, 1979

Age at time of recording: 27

Bass: '70s Musicman Stingray

Amp: Recorded direct into the mixing console

Good Times

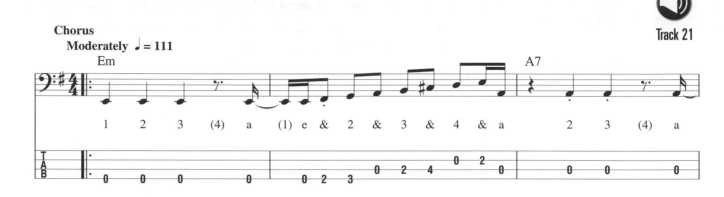

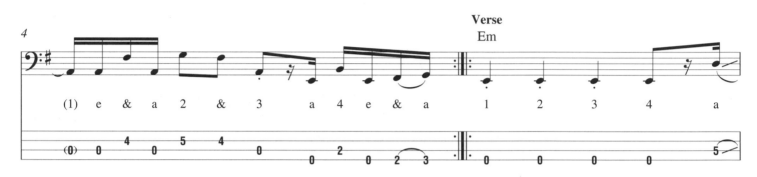

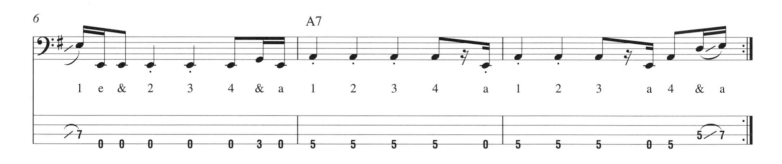

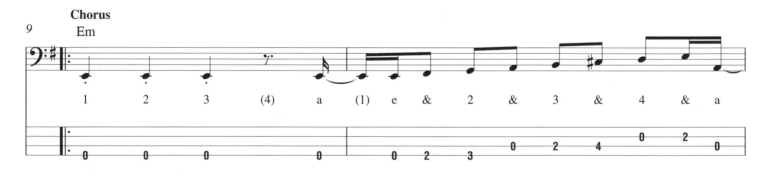

Words and Music by Nile Rodgers and Bernard Edwards
Copyright © 1979 Sony/ATV Music Publishing LLC and Bernard's Other Music
All Rights on behalf of Sony/ATV Music Publishing LLC Administered by Sony/ATV Music Publishing LLC, 8 Music Square West, Nashville, TN 37203
International Copyright Secured   All Rights Reserved

John Deacon

"Another One Bites the Dust" is one of the biggest songs ever released by the English rock band Queen. Written by bass player John Deacon and featured on the group's album *The Game* in 1980, it became a worldwide crossover hit, going to #1 on the US Billboard Hot 100, #2 on the R&B charts, and #7 on the UK Singles Chart. Sales have exceeded seven million copies.

Formed in 1970, Queen consisted of vocalist Freddie Mercury, guitarist Brian May, bassist John Deacon, and drummer Roger Taylor. One of the biggest bands of all time, their hits songs, originality, and live showmanship have put them in a league all their own. In 1985, their Live Aid show was voted the best live rock

"Let's just say that the product of drummer Roger Taylor and bassist John Deacon is explosive— a colossal sonic volcano whose eruption maketh the earth tremble."
—Gordon Fletcher,
Rolling Stone music critic

performance of all time, and they've sold over 300 million albums worldwide.

Early success came for the band in the seventies with the albums *Queen* and *Queen II*. But they became worldwide stars with *Sheer Heart Attack* (1974) and *A Night at the Opera* (1975). In 1991, Freddie Mercury passed away, and in 1999, John Deacon retired. Since then, Brian May and Roger Taylor have performed occasionally at various

special events. They did team up with Bad Company singer Paul Rodgers for several years, but Rodgers never formally joined the band.

The bass line was actually inspired by Chic's "Good Times" (see "Good Times"). Bernard Edwards (Chic bassist) stated in an interview with *New Musical Express*, "...that Queen record came about because that Queen bass player... spent some time hanging out with us at

© Marty Temme

our

QUEEN
The Game

This is one of the hardest Queen songs to understand. "Steve walks warily down the street, his brim pulled way down low. Ain't no sound but the sound of his feet, machine gun ready to go." Also, the last phrase is not "shoot her," but "shoot out."

studio." Soon after "Good Times" was recorded, Queen started working on *The Game* in 1980 with producer Reinhold Mack.

"Another One Bites the Dust" was tracked at Musicland Studios in Munich, West Germany. John Deacon played bass, piano, guitars, and handclap percussion. Roger Taylor created a drum loop. Brian May contributed guitar effects with an Eventide Harmonizer. No synthesizers were used; all effects are created with pianos, guitars, drums, and reverse tape playback. Queen didn't even consider the song to be a single until pop star Michael Jackson suggested it. Good thing they listened; it became wildly successful and was even nominated for a Grammy. The song is built around that punchy, irresistible bass line created and played by John Deacon on his recently acquired Musicman Stingray bass.

This bass line is one of the most recognizable lines in music. At Los

Angeles Dodgers games, it is heard when opponents strike out. During the Gulf War, the American Military radio stations would often play this when a Scud missile was shot down. In Australian Cricket, the chorus of the song comes on when a batsman gets out. Years after Freddie Mercury died, Wyclef Jean remixed the song for the 1998 movie *Small Soldiers*. This version also appeared on Queen's compilation *Greatest Hits III* released in 1999.

How to Play It

If you want to sound *exactly* like John Deacon when you play "Another One Bites the Dust," then pay attention to the tablature in the notation example for this song. If you try to play this by relying on the open A and D strings, you will never *feel* the groove. Your job is to *connect* each chord in perfect time. Your job is also to cleanly articulate each note as you *sit* inside each chord.

Hint: If you can sing it, you can play it

Put your bass down, and sing the bass part along with the recording. Be attentive to pronouncing each note with your tongue. Staccato each phonetic with your tongue where you see staccato signs in the notation. After you can really sing the part, pick up your bass and try to *sing* the bass part with your fingers.

If you want to get your notes to staccato, you will have to immediately *mute* each note with your plucking fingers *and* your fretting fingers. This two-handed combo technique will give great results. Take your time to get your fingers and hands synchronized. This technique can be mastered easily if you take your time and really focus on the job at hand.

At the pre-chorus, the song appears to reference the relative major (G), and the bass moves with the chords and plays roots. The bass leads the charge. Think of the A and B chords at the end as the IV and V chords of E minor. If you do this, you will *intuit* the return to E minor. Many songs move seamlessly between the relative major and minor chords as tonic centers for verses, B sections, choruses, and bridges. Keep your ears open, and you'll recognize these tone center shifts. Even though you never really modulate to another key in the song, the shift from relative minor to major and vice versa creates that illusion.

Vital Stats

Bassist: John Deacon

Song: "Another One Bites the Dust"

Album: *The Game* – Queen, 1980

Age at time of recording: 29

Bass: Late '70s Musicman Stingray bass

Amp: The bass was recorded direct into the mixing console

Track 22

Sara Lee

The B-52s

"Sara Lee's groove on 'Love Shack' is the very reason everyone wanted to dance to that record. She grooves on everything she plays on."

—Pete Thompson, drummer for Robin Trower

The B-52's started out as a new wave rock band from Athens, Georgia. Presenting as a positive, enthusiastic, slightly wacky party band, the B-52's hits include "Rock Lobster," "Girl from Ipanema Goes to Greenland," and "Love Shack." All their tunes are set to a danceable new wave beat.

In 1989 they made a brilliant decision when then hired Nile Rodgers and Don Was to produce their album, *Cosmic Thing*. Those guys know how to make a song groove. As a writing partner/ guitarist in Chic along with the brilliant bassist Bernard Edwards, Nile Rodgers proved beyond all doubt that he can play funk guitar, which he does on "Love Shack." And Don Was is an excellent bassist/arranger/producer in his own right. When the two of them work on an album, it's going to be a hit.

Cosmic Thing was a smash for the B-52's, and "Love Shack" hit #3 on the Billboard Hot 100. The groove propelled "Love Shack" to dance classic status. The bass part is so simple, yet so irresistible. The song's inspiration was a tin roof cabin near Athens, Georgia. B-52's singer

"Love Shack" introduced the B-52s to a mainstream audience. They had a strong cult following, especially in the gay community, but not a broad audience until this song became a hit.

Kate Pierson lived in the cabin in the seventies, and the cabin existed until it burned down in 2004.

Bassist Sara Lee was born in the West Midlands of England. Her parents were music teachers, and music formed an important part of her childhood. She played tympani and double bass in school as a teenager, until she discovered the electric bass guitar. She moved to London and worked as a secretary at Polydor Records where she was discovered by King Crimson leader Robert Fripp. She went on to work with Robyn Hitchcock and famed punk band Gang of Four in England, and later moved to the United States.

After she moved to the US, her reputation for "delivering good grooves and staying in the pocket" earned her steady work, and Sara became an in-demand session and touring bass player, eventually hired to play on the B-52's *Cosmic Thing* album. Following a gig supporting the tour, Sara formed the Raging Hormones with B-52's session drummer Charley Drayton. She then played with the Indigo Girls for seven years. In 1996 and 1997, she toured with singer-songwriter Ani DiFranco throughout Europe and North America.

Other artists who have hired Sara Lee include Joan Osborne, Ryuichi Sakamoto, and Fiona Apple. Sara re-joined the B-52's as a touring member in 1999. She released her debut solo album *Make It Beautiful* on Difranco's Righteous Babe records in 2000. The album features funky bass lines worked out over twenty years of her bass playing career. Sara was also a judge for the Fifth Annual Independent Music Awards to support independent artists' careers.

How to Play It

I like to call this a bass line made from a "funky arpeggio." In this case, it's a C7 chord. The important "landing notes" are chord tones (C/root, E/major 3rd, G/5th, and B♭/♭7th). Then there are "passing notes" between these chord tones that help to flesh out the groove. The coolest thing you can do on a bass guitar is to recognize that in the key of C, the move to the low 3rd (the open E) has incredible harmonic impact. Try it for yourself and you will surely agree.

The chorus pedals roots of chords C, E♭, F, and A♭. The cool thing is that, rather than continue up the register to a higher F and A♭, Sara opts for the low F and A♭. No question about it, Sara Lee can groove with the best of them.

Vital Stats

Bassist: Sara Lee

Song: "Love Shack"

Album: *Cosmic Thing –* The B-52s, 1989

Bass: G&L L-2000

Amp: Recorded direct into the mixing console

Love Shack

Verse
Moderate fast Rock ♩ = 132

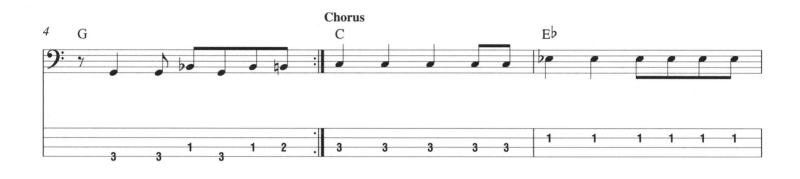

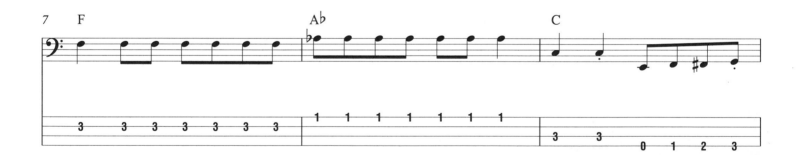

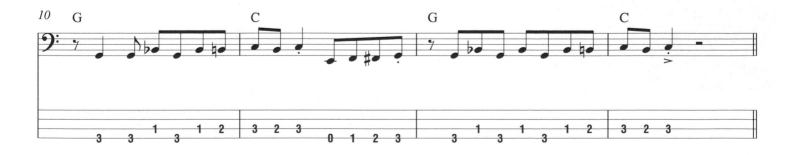

Words and Music by Catherine E. Pierson, Frederick W. Schneider, Keith J. Strickland and Cynthia L. Wilson

Flea

"I like hearing the bass when it's really locking in with the drums. I like it simple. I like it when it makes you want to have sex— that warm, good feeling."

—Flea

"Aeroplane" is based on a traditional blues song called "Jesus Is My Aeroplane." On their Greatest Hits DVD, the Red Hot Chili Peppers explain that is how they feel about music… that it takes them to a higher place.

"Aeroplane," from the 1995 album, *One Hot Minute*, is one of the funkiest tunes recorded by the Red Hot Chili Peppers. Though the song was not included on their *Greatest Hits* CD, bassists have been drawn to this song since its release. Despite its dark lyrics, the groove, driven by a funk slap bass line, is irresistible. Paradoxically to the lyrics, the melodies are actually upbeat, aided by child chorus vocals from Flea's daughter, Clara, and her schoolmates.

The Red Hot Chili Peppers formed in Los Angeles, CA in 1983. They began as an alternative rock band, but over the years have fused traditional rock and funk with elements of punk and pop. Current band members include Anthony Kiedis on vocals, Josh Klinghoffer on guitar, Chad Smith on drums, and Michael "Flea" Balzary on bass. The Chili Peppers have won seven Grammies and sold over 50 million albums worldwide.

"Aeroplane" is based on a traditional blues song called "Jesus Is My Aeroplane." Some of the lyrics seem to be about hedonism and drug use—notably the

© Marty Temme

refrain "I like pleasure spiked with pain." What sets this song apart is really the funk groove, driven by Flea's bass, plain and simple.

Flea was born in Australia in 1962. Aside from the Red Hot Chili Peppers, he's worked with many artists, including Alanis Morissette, Jane's Addiction, and the Mars Volta. His roots are in funk and punk. Though known for his in-your-face style, Flea considers his style to be minimalist while using complexity in moderation.

Originally a trumpet prodigy, Flea learned to play bass in high school from close friend and original Red Hot Chili Peppers guitarist Hillel Slovak. He joined Hillel to form an impromptu collaboration that would ultimately give birth to the Red Hot Chili Peppers. When it comes to creative energy, musical philosophy, and overall style, Flea would be the first to call himself a punk rocker before a funk legend. His infusion of punk into the slap funk playing style of Louis Johnson and Larry Graham has turned the next generation of rock fans to funk bass.

To quote Flea about his beginnings, "In high school, I saw some guy slapping on a bass, and I thought, 'Wow, that's cool.' So I started doing it." He quickly developed a style of his own and he taught himself the bass. However, he admits there are drawbacks to teaching yourself how to play: "I can sight-read classical trumpet music really well, but I can't read a note of bass music. And, as far as economy of movement is concerned, I don't have that down at all."

He continues, "When I slap, I slam the strings as hard as I can with my thumb; I use only my middle finger—never my index or ring fingers—to pop. If the part is very intricate, I use mostly a wrist motion, but usually it involves the whole arm. I've seen people slap and hardly move their hand at all, but anyone who's ever seen one of our shows knows that's not me! I believe if I get my whole body into it, I can play better."

No doubt, Flea is a unique player. Without question, his bass playing style is special and has influenced a generation of bass players. He plays 100 percent from the heart. With or without "proper" technique, Flea is a great bass player, and his playing on "Aeroplane" is a world-class performance. An analysis will give us a glimpse into what makes up a slap routine that is 100 percent groove.

How to Play It

The song is a lesson in itself about how to play slap bass. If you can master the technique Flea uses here, then you are *there*. There are fancier ways to slap, including the use of triplets, back-and-forth thumb plucks, or even fret-hand percussive tapping that calls and answers to the slapping hand. All those are impressive in a concert setting. The bass player will blow everyone's mind for sure, but it is "all flash and no smash," as Lonnie Marshall of Weapon of Choice so aptly put it. For my money, the slap groove to the verse of "Aeroplane" is what slap and pop bass *should* be all about—vibe and groove. It's got a nasty badass vibe, and it sits deep in the pocket.

Flea explains how he came up with the part: "I was sitting in my garage with a bass Louis Johnson gave me—a Treker Louis Johnson Signature 4-string—and I started playing that seventies funk line. The bass had light strings on it and had that whacka-whackita sound. It's kind of a 'been done' groove, but it's nice, and Anthony liked it. Actually, 'Aeroplane' was the only song on the album I was

worried about—I thought it sounded like another stupid white boy trying to be funky! [laughs]."

The secret to being able to play this part is the slap technique. Flea's slapping hand *never stops keeping time*. You do not have to strike a string every time your hand moves, but all the notes are there within that up and down motion of the slapping hand. It's as simple (and as complicated) as that.

Let's make an analogy to pick-style playing. The best pick-style playing is when you play downbeat notes (notes on beats 1, 2, 3, 4) with downstrokes and upbeat notes (1 + 2 + 3 + 4 +) with upstrokes. If you're playing sixteenth notes, double-time the concept. If you approach this song with this knowledge, the technique will magically appear.

It will actually surprise you how easy and relaxed the part is to play. At first, it will feel awkward, and you'll feel like the whitest bass player on Earth. But keep at it and don't give up; you'll find yourself stumbling into the groove and, low and behold, you will be flying in that "Aeroplane."

Vital Stats

Bassist: Flea

Song: "Aeroplane"

Album: *One Hot Minute –* Red Hot Chili Peppers, 1995

Age at time of recording: 33

Bass: Ernie Ball Musicman Stingray 4-string bass

Amp: Recorded direct into the mixing console

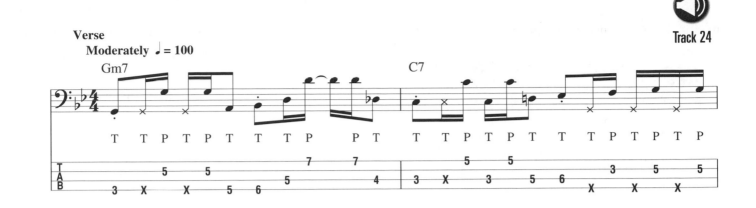

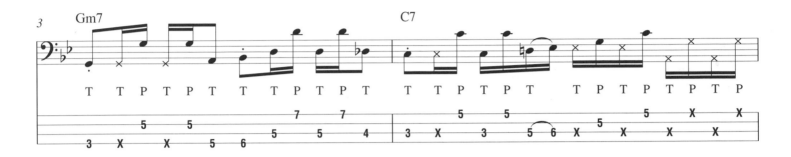

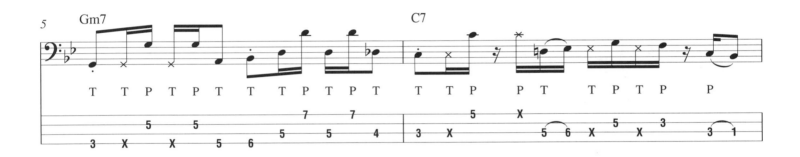

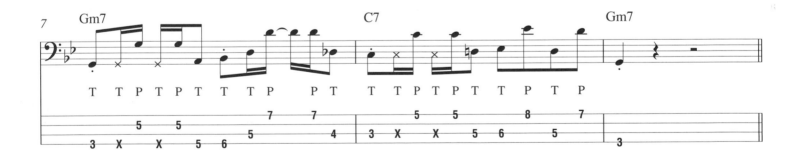

Glenn Letsch

Photo by Neil Calendra

"No Time" is a song recorded and played in concert by British guitar legend Robin Trower. Robin was born in 1945 in England. In 1962, he formed the Paramounts, which later included high school pal, Gary Brooker. The band broke up in 1966, but a year later, Robin joined Gary's new group, Procol Harum ("Whiter Shade of Pale"), where he remained until 1972 when he decided to go solo.

Before starting his namesake band, Robin worked with singer Frankie Miller, bass player James Dewar, and Jethro Tull drummer, Clive Bunker. They were called Jude. They played a few gigs that were very well received, but they never made an album and quickly broke up. James Dewar continued to work with Robin. Drummer Reg Isadore came on board, and the Robin Trower Band was officially formed in 1973. *Bridge of Sighs* is their most famous album. Recorded in 1974, it was produced by Matthew Fisher (organist for Procol Harum).

In the early eighties, Robin formed BLT with Jack Bruce (see "Sunshine of Your Love") and drummer Bill Lordan. By the end of the decade, Robin had added Davey Pattison on vocals, Dave Bronze on bass, and Pete Thompson on drums. They recorded the album *Passion*, which featured the studio version of the dreamy laid back shuffle, "No Time." In 2007, Robin released a third recording called *Seven Moons*.

Robin Trower toured the United States and Canada in the summer and autumn of 2006. A 2008 world tour began in Ft. Pierce, Florida in January, and joining

Davey Pattison and Pete Thompson was Glenn Letsch playing bass. European dates began in April. The band released the live album *RT @ RO in 08*. The band continues to tour and has plans to release a new studio album in 2010.

Glenn has played with many of rock's luminaries including Gamma (featuring Ronnie Montrose), Gregg Allman, Neal Schon, Johnny Colla (Huey Lewis & the News), Montrose, and New Frontier. He's the featured session bassist on *The Sims* computer games and numerous television commercials. He recently completed albums for singer Eddie Money as well as the *Barack Obama Tribute* album for iTunes.

Glenn is a published author of bass instructional textbooks for Hal Leonard Publishing and Alfred Publishing. His books include *Stuff! Good Bass Players Should Know*, *Hal Leonard R&B Bass Method*, *Hal Leonard Country Bass Method*, *Bass for Beginners*, *Glenn Letsch's Bass Masters Class*, *Bass Lessons for the Greats*, and *James Brown Bass Signature Licks*. His Hot Licks Videos bass video, *The Lowdown with Glenn Letsch*, received an A+ rating from *Bass Player* magazine.

> *"Time, space, and groove—these are the three elements needed when playing bass. You must be able to play in time. You must leave space so your part breathes. And you must groove by making your part feel great to play and listen to."*
>
> —Glenn Letsch

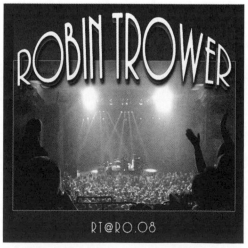

RT @RO in 08 was recorded live during a single concert at the Royal Oak Theater in Detroit, MI. Recorded near the end of a 50-city tour, there were no overdubs or repairs performed during the post-production of this album.

"No Time" is a mainstay of the Robin Trower concert set list and can be heard on his latest live album, *RT @ RO in 08*. It features the blue-eyed soul singing of Scotsman Davey Pattison, the masterfully dreamy hi-hat and cymbals of Pete Thompson, Glenn Letsch's combination guitar and bass accompaniment, and the inimitable guitar of Robin Trower. Atmospheric and deep grooving with a soaring guitar solo and passionate R&B influenced vocalizing, "No Time" is the perfect combination only realized to full potential in the live concert setting.

How to Play It

This song is played in physical E on the bass and guitar, but is actually in concert D. That is to say, the bass and guitar have been tuned down a whole step from standard pitch. This is the choice of guitarist Robin Trower for a few reasons, but most notably, it allows for ease of bending heavy gauge strings (which he uses). Additionally, the lower key has a more mystical dreamy tonality, which works for Robin Trower's music. For ease of discussion, we will refer to the key of E for "No Time."

The chord sequence for the solo is Em7–A7–C–Em7, which is the same as the verses. During the verses, the bass plays a routine based on the E tonality, and the guitar handles the chords. However, during the solo, Robin cannot play the chords *and* the solo.

In a power trio, when the chords stop on the guitar, there's no one to pick up the slack. The bass usually does its thing, while the guitar player rips a solo. In "No Time," if the bass were to continue outlining the tonic Em7 chord, there would be no chord progression to accompany the soloist. There would be a gaping whole in the soundscape. How do you fix that? The bass must play the chords. But what happens to the bass part? The bass player better keep that going, too. How does one play the chords *and* the bass at the same time? Listen to the CD example for "No Time" and read the notation and tablature, because the bass *is* playing the bass part *and* the chords at the same time. It can be done, and you can do it.

The bass routine is played on the E and A string, while the chord routine is played on the D and G strings. The chord is struck on beat 2 in every other measure. You must rake across both the D and the G strings quickly with one finger, as if it were one fat string, so the two notes of the chord sound simultaneously. Keep your fret-hand fingers down so the chord can sustain, but you must continue pedaling the low E while the chord rings out *and* also pluck the G to A move on the A string to keep the bass routine going.

The first chord is an Em7—play D on the D string and G on the G string at the 12th fret. D is the flat 7th and G is the minor 3rd of Em7. The second chord is A7. Play the C♯ at fret 11 on the D string—it is the major 3rd of A7. Play G on the G string at fret 12, which is the flat 7th of A7. The third chord is C. Play C on the D string at fret 10—the root of the chord. Play G on the G string at fret 12—the perfect 5th of the C chord. The fourth chord is the same as the first chord: Em7. Play it the same way.

The second time through the chord sequence, move up the neck to play the new voicing of each chord. Do not forget to keep the bass part going while the chords sustain. You will have to experiment with different finger choices to see what works best for you.

Again, the first chord is an Em7. This time play E on the D string at the 14th fret—the root of the chord. Play B on the G string at the 16th fret—the 5th of the chord. The second chord is A7. Play the G on the 17th fret of the D string. It is the flat 7th of A7. Play C♯ on the G string at the 18th fret. It is the major 3rd of the A7 chord. The third chord is C. Play G on the D string at fret 17—the 5th of the chord. Play C on the G string at fret 17—the root of the C chord. The fourth chord is again Em7, but this time with a new arpeggiated voicing. Play G on the D string at fret 17—the minor 3rd of the chord. Next pluck D on the G string at fret 19, which is the flat 7th of the chord. Then rake down and pluck E on the A string at fret 19—the root of the chord. Continue raking into low open E.

Aside from these cool chords, what really makes this cool is the bass part *never* stops. What makes it even cooler is that it never stops outlining the tonic Em7 chord. So there is major tension created by pedaling a low E against an A7 and a C chord. *That* is the coolest thing about the whole song.

Vital Stats

Bassist: Glenn Letsch

Song: "No Time"

Album: *RT @ RO in 08* – Robin Trower, 2008

Age at time of recording: 59

Bass: Glenn Letsch Pipemaster Custom bass

Amp: Direct feed to the console

Track 25

Tune down 1 step:
(low to high) D–G–C–F

Guitar Solo
Slow Blues ♩ = 84

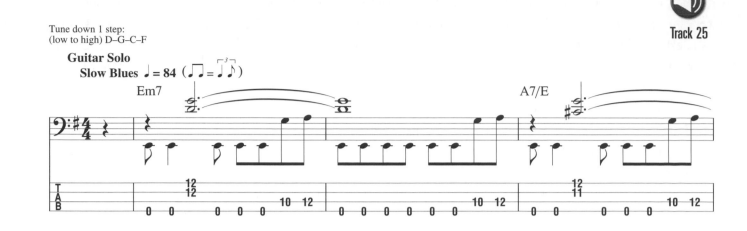

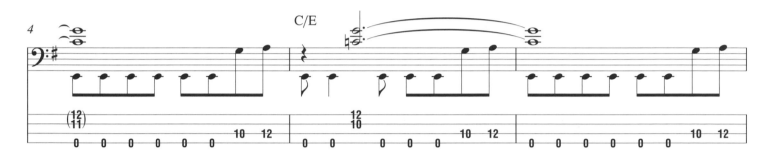

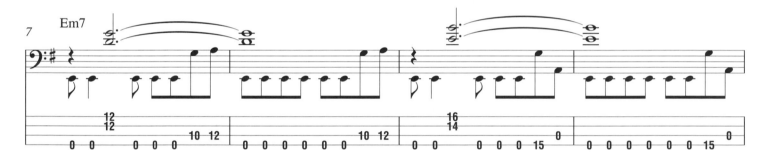

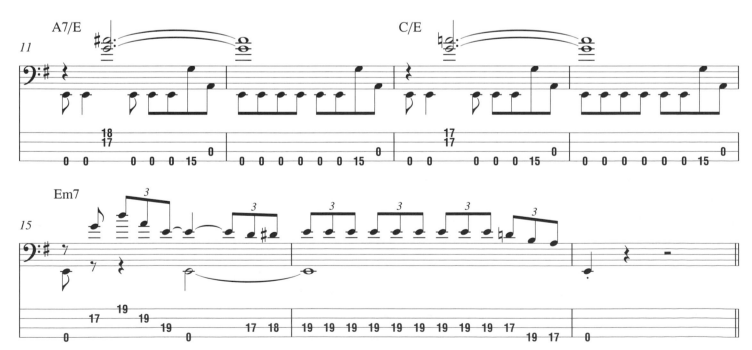

Words and Music by David Bronze, Robin Trower and Reginald Webb

Conclusion

Thanks for taking the journey through *25 Great Bass Lines*. The intention is that you do indeed learn and master each and every song in this book. Paul McCartney of the Beatles, James Jamerson of Motown, Jack Bruce from Cream, the Meters' George Porter, Jr., Bootsy Collins from James Brown, David Hood of Muscle Shoals, Bernard Edwards of Chic—these cats were brilliant pioneers. They paved the way for everyone else with their taste, creativity, and ability to take over a song without detracting from the song. Listening to these bass lines is easy; the tough part is dedicating yourself to mastering them. "Kinda sorta" playing the part is not enough—it takes blood, sweat, and tears. But those tears will be tears of joy for what you accomplish.

About the Author

Photo by Neil Calendra

Glenn Letsch's musical career spans over 30 years. As a professional bassist, he has recorded countless albums and toured worldwide. He has graced the concert stage with the likes of Robin Trower, Gamma, Montrose, Gregg Allman, Jonathan Cain, and Neal Schon, among many others.

His acclaimed instructional video *Bass Guitar: The Lowdown with Glenn Letsch* (Hot Licks Videos) was rated A+ by *Bass Player* magazine. His first book, *Bass Lessons with the Greats*, was hailed by *Bass Player* magazine as "the best instructional text since *Standing in the Shadows of Motown*." His second book, *Glenn Letsch's Bass Masters Class* is a perennial seller for Hal Leonard Corporation, as is its follow-up, *Bass for Beginners: The Complete Guide*. Additionally, Glenn has written *R&B Bass*, the definitive source for Motown, Stax, Atlantic, and James-Brown style bass playing; *Country Bass*, a similar work for country bass styles; *Stuff! Good Bass Players Should Know—An A-Z Guide to Getting Better; James Brown Bass Signature Licks* was recently published and is the definitive analysis of the great James Brown bass lines.

Glenn also played bass for the computer game series *The Sims*, the No. 1 selling computer game in the world today. He has also been a featured "Woodshed" columnist for *Bass Player* magazine, in which he offers unique instructional methods for the aspiring bassist.

Be sure to check out Glenn's website, *www.glennletsch.com*. There you will find valuable playing tips as well as information about Glenn's custom line of basses. You can email Glenn at *glenn@glennletsch.com*.

BASS NOTATION LEGEND

Bass music can be notated two different ways: on a *musical staff*, and in *tablature*.

THE MUSICAL STAFF shows pitches and rhythms and is divided by bar lines into measures. Pitches are named after the first seven letters of the alphabet.

TABLATURE graphically represents the bass fingerboard. Each horizontal line represents a string, and each number represents a fret.

3rd string, open   2nd string, 2nd fret   1st & 2nd strings open, played together

HAMMER-ON: Strike the first (lower) note with one finger, then sound the higher note (on the same string) with another finger by fretting it without picking.

PULL-OFF: Place both fingers on the notes to be sounded. Strike the first note and without picking, pull the finger off to sound the second (lower) note.

LEGATO SLIDE: Strike the first note and then slide the same fret-hand finger up or down to the second note. The second note is not struck.

SHIFT SLIDE: Same as legato slide, except the second note is struck.

TRILL: Very rapidly alternate between the notes indicated by continuously hammering on and pulling off.

TREMOLO PICKING: The note is picked as rapidly and continuously as possible.

VIBRATO: The string is vibrated by rapidly bending and releasing the note with the fretting hand.

SHAKE: Using one finger, rapidly alternate between two notes on one string by sliding either a half-step above or below.

NATURAL HARMONIC: Strike the note while the fret hand lightly touches the string directly over the fret indicated.

MUFFLED STRINGS: A percussive sound is produced by laying the fret hand across the string(s) without depressing them and striking them with the pick hand.

BEND: Strike the note and bend up the interval shown.

BEND AND RELEASE: Strike the note and bend up as indicated, then release back to the original note. Only the first note is struck.

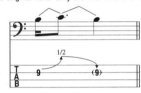

RIGHT-HAND TAP: Hammer ("tap") the fret indicated with the "pick-hand" index or middle finger and pull off to the note fretted by the fret hand.

LEFT-HAND TAP: Hammer ("tap") the fret indicated with the "fret-hand" index or middle finger.

SLAP: Strike ("slap") string with right-hand thumb.

POP: Snap ("pop") string with right-hand index or middle finger.

Additional Musical Definitions

> (accent) • Accentuate note (play it louder).

^ (accent) • Accentuate note with great intensity.

. (staccato) • Play the note short.

⊓ • Downstroke

∨ • Upstroke

D.S. al Coda • Go back to the sign (𝄋), then play until the measure marked "***To Coda***," then skip to the section labelled "Coda."

D.C. al Fine • Go back to the beginning of the song and play until the measure marked "***Fine***" (end).

Bass Fig. • Label used to recall a recurring pattern.

Fill • Label used to identify a brief melodic figure which is to be inserted into the arrangement.

tacet • Instrument is silent (drops out).

• Repeat measures between signs.

1. | 2. • When a repeated section has different endings, play the first ending only the first time and the second ending only the second time.

NOTE: Tablature numbers in parentheses mean:
    1. The note is being sustained over a system (note in standard notation is tied), or
    2. The note is sustained, but a new articulation (such as a hammer-on, pull-off, slide or vibrato) begins.